What's in Your Boat House?

WHAT'S IN YOUR BOAT HOUSE?

Amazing Stories of Nautical Archaeology

Bob Matson

With a Foreword by Dennis Evinrude

North Star Press of St. Cloud, Inc.
St. Cloud, Minnesota

Cover photo by *National Geographic* photographer Jim Brandenburg (www.jimbrandenburg.com).

Cover design by Matt Smith—Smith-Gifford Advertising.

ISBN 978-0-87839-695-5

First Edition: June 2013

Printed in the United States of America

Published by
North Star Press of St. Cloud, Inc.
P.O. Box 451
St. Cloud, Minnesota 56302

northstarpress.com

Dedication

I look up and I see God. I look down and see my dog. G-O-D – D-O-G.

It may seem silly to dedicate a book to a dog, but that's what I'm going to do.

Cedar

As a single person, writing a book can be a daunting, lonely task. Yet, I have had the warm and comforting presence of this loyal Labrador by my side every minute of the day. In fact, Cedar was never more than a few feet away while writing this book. His eyes never looked elsewhere, just right at me, trying to decipher my every click of the keyboard.

If every human being on this earth would be as loving, loyal and faithful as this gorgeous animal, life on this planet would be utopia.

Life is so fleeting for dogs. They bless us for a time, and then they are gone. Cedar died in my arms in February of 2011 during the completion of this book. I look up and I see God. I look down and see my dog. May you live forever, Cedar, through this book. I love you.

Foreword

By Dennis Evinrude
President (retired) Antique Outboard Motor Club

AS A STUDENT I CARED nothing for history. My spare time was occupied by a love for anything mechanical, especially if it consumed fossil fuel. I was interested in fast cars, airplanes, and eventually boats and outboard motors. I am sure being related to Ole and Bess Evinrude, pioneers of outboards, was the spark that ignited my interest in watercraft. A number of years ago I started collecting old outboards and purchased several wooden boats as well as one classic aluminum boat. Many people are astounded to find out that there are collectors of old outboard motors. What drives someone to collect? There are of course a few people in every hobby that are mercenary in nature and are in it strictly for profit. While collectors sometimes look down on profiteers, they often serve to seek out and find the very items we need for restorations. I believe the motivation for the rest of us is a sense of history. That craving for the history of things I collected was slowly awakened in me and became the most important component in my love of antique and classic outboards and boats. That sense of history has more than one facet. For many collectors it can be hard to determine what's the more rewarding part of the collection process. You start by hearing a rumor about an object of interest. Your heartbeat quickens and adrenaline rushes to your chest. Days and weeks, sometimes months and years, pass before you can acquire the rumored find. Now comes the discovery of the history. You ask questions of anybody who might know something about your new-found treasure or can send you off in the correct direction. You are researching at the same pace you might for a college paper. Ultimately, you're able to restore the boat and motor and are rightfully proud of what you've accomplished. So what part was the most fun?

It may be different for every collector. Thankfully the end result is the same. We have a fun piece of history preserved for generations to come. I happen to be a rider of a Harley Davidson motorcycle. There's a saying among Harley riders that speaks to the question, "What is the mystique all about?" The answer, often seen on shirts, is "If I have to explain it, you wouldn't understand." If you don't understand the mystique of collecting old boats and motors, Bob's book is perfect for you. In the pages that follow, Bob has assembled many accounts of the process I've described. I suspect most who read this will already have an interest in the hunt and the satisfaction of the finished product. May you also come to realize the importance of the history associated with each restored treasure. Then you'll be able to say, "I understand the mystique. I get it!"

Contents

Introduction

By Bob Matson

I HAVE TO ADMIT that the inspiration for this book came from a book about cars. I'm an avid car enthusiast, coming from a car family. I have owned a 1958 Edsel, a 1976 Rolls Royce Silver Shadow, and my current collectible is a 1967 Land Rover Safari Estate Wagon. When I read Tom Cotter's two books, *The Cobra in the Barn* and *The Hemi in the Barn*, I got to thinking about how many secluded boathouses (or barns for that matter) might be harboring some fantastic old boats.

You see, I own Matson Motors, a marine and small engine business at the headquarters of the Boundary Waters Canoe Area Wilderness, in Ely, Minnesota. About 250 lakes in a twenty-five-mile radius surround Ely, so I figured there must be some real finds out there, just in my immediate area. In my business, I specialize in restoring vintage outboards and boats for customers, and have heard hundreds of times, "We've had this old motor in our family for years. We would like to hear it run again." I knew this could be true for boats too, but how to find such stories I had no clue. I did know that the Internet would be a great source, and I put out notices on websites like retrocrestliner.com and the Antique Outboard Motor Club, Inc. website. I also networked with a number of outboard collectors I knew, and soon the stories started to come in. I can already see a sequel to this book, and if you have such a story, I would like to hear from you at www.whatsinyourboathouse.com.

My enthusiasm for this book really ramped up after my own incredible "find," and all of the coincidences surrounding its restoration. I knew I had the first chapter.

So sit back and enjoy . . . you'll never look at an old boathouse the same way again!

Ready to launch.

My Quest for a Crestliner

By Bob Matson

My search for a boat was brought about by a need. My daily driver was a Jeep Wrangler that could not pull my heavy fiberglass Crestliner Apollo. Therefore, the boat had to be left up in Nestor Falls, Ontario. I own a cabin on an island ten miles out of Nestor, on the Lake of the Woods. Since I couldn't pull the heavy boat back to Ely, I had no boat to use on my lake at home. I live on beautiful Cedar Lake near Ely. My plan was to sell the old fiberglass boat and buy a new light-weight aluminum boat I could tow back and forth. My plan for the new boat—maybe a Lund or Crestline. But as I started restoring other people's vintage boats, I fell in love with the classic lines, durability and the attention they commanded from on-lookers. I said to myself, "Wait a minute. I don't need a new boat. I need a classic restored boat that would get me to my island, as well as act as a marketing tool for my restoration business."

I began advertising for a boat like this, but I knew my best bet would be on Internet sites like Ebay and Craig's List. Then, I discovered a website devoted to Crestliners. After looking at other people's boats, I knew that I wanted one of these. **First coincidence:** The Matsons of Duluth, Minnesota (No relation), owned Retrocrestliner.com!

After looking at many different models of vintage Crestliners, I thought an eighteen-foot Voyageur would be just what I needed. It could haul all my stuff out to the island, which would include food, clothing, fishing gear, tools, and sometimes even furniture!

My chances of finding such a boat seemed dim, especially after monitoring the websites for months to no avail. Then, there it was! Up came a 1958 Crestliner eighteen-foot Voyageur with trailer, no motor. It looked to be in pretty nice shape. I knew I had to have this one. In my mind, I immediately budgeted $500 for gas to go to some distant state to pick it up. I closed my eyes, scrolled to the bottom of the screen, and then opened them to see how far I had to go. **Coincidence number two:** Whoa! It was located in Virginia, Minnesota, only forty-three miles from Ely! I promised myself I just wouldn't be out-bid on this boat! But, I knew nothing about how to do the bidding process on Ebay. **Coincidence number Three:** The next day, a good friend and customer of mine from Indiana was up for a visit and stopped at my shop. We got to talking about boats, and I told him about my find on Ebay, and that I was afraid I'd lose it because I didn't know very much about bidding.

He said to me, "That's how I make my living, buying and selling things on Ebay. I'll do it for you!"

Bingo! I gave him my bid parameters, and within a few hours I had won the bid. After contacting the owner by phone, we agreed I could come to Virginia that weekend to pick it up. I spent several sleepless nights pouring over pictures of the boat I had printed off the website.

I knew that I wanted to completely restore it and that I had to do it right. It was to be an example of how I would do customers' boats. I also knew this would take time, and I wanted to get started right away.

I arrived at the owner's house, introduced myself and wrote out a check for the agreed amount. The boat sat in his yard, somewhat worse for wear and tear. I looked it over carefully and noticed that it didn't have a dent anywhere on the sides or bottom hull. When I expressed my delight, the owner said, "That's because I just bought it from a guy from Superior, and he'd stored it in a boathouse for forty years. It's never bumped a dock or hit the bottom!"

"Why are you selling it?" I asked?

He said, "Well, my intention was to restore it, but I no sooner got it here when the transmission went out on my van. My wife says I have to sell it to pay for the repairs." (One man's misery is another man's delight!)

My next goal was to look at the trailer it sat on. It looked pretty substantial and had funny-looking homemade square fenders. I knew nothing about trailers at this point, but I did like the fact that it had both coil springs and shock absorbers. We said our goodbyes, and I headed off for Ely. On the way back I noticed how easy it was for my Jeep to tow it, and how the boat seemed to float over the bumps. I knew then that trailering it to Canada was going to be easy. I was really happy.

This is how she looked on my first day of ownership.

One thing I was sure of. I wanted the aluminum sides to be highly polished, and I wanted to paint the rest of the boat black to match my Jeep. I spent all day Sunday on the Internet, researching how to polish the boat to a bright finish. I saw this was a three-grit, wet-sanding process, and that it was going to take hours of elbow grease.

On Monday, I parked the boat in front of my shop, right in front of my big windows. I was standing there, looking at it and thinking about the restoration process and of how much work polishing the aluminum was going to be. Just then, a guy walked in the front door and asked if I had any older outboards he could buy. I said I had one older eighteen-horsepower Evinrude that ran well, for $350. He said he would be interested in looking at it, so I went out back and dragged it in. While he looked it over, I asked him his name and did he work in Ely? **Coincidence number Four:** He said, "I just opened up a new business in the former city garages. I specialize in restoring aluminum anything and professional painting."

I couldn't believe my ears! I said, "Have I got a deal for you! I'll barter the Evinrude if you polish the sides of my boat!"

He agreed, and now I had the hardest part of the restoration process taken care of. His name's Matt, and he does quality work. In fact, I had planned to paint the boat myself, but once I saw a classic pickup truck he was painting, I said, "Oh, Matt, you have to paint my boat, too. I'll pay you for that." So now, within one day, I had two of the time-consuming jobs already underway. I was months ahead of schedule.

While the boat was at Matt's shop, I had the trailer at my shop. I poured over the trailer looking for a brand name but could find no vin number or manufacture's plate. But, it did have a distinctive design, so I figured the Interne%t would help. It sure did! It identified the trailer as a Tee Nee Trailer, built in Youngstown, Ohio. Tee Nee trailers are collectible in their own right. They are known for their bright yellow color and teardrop shaped fenders. I decided to have the trailer sandblasted and painted yellow, of course, but I did wish it had those tear drop fenders.

Coincidence number Five: I had attended Dan Wyman's Antique Outboard meet in Clouquet, Minnesota, a year earlier. While there, I struck up a conversation with Dan about members. He talked about how good the turnout was for his meet, but wished Del had shown up from Osseo, Minnesota, with his fenders. I asked, what kind of fenders? "Oh, he makes fiberglass reproduction Tee Nee Trailer fenders." When I returned home, I immediately e-mailed Del, and sure enough, he said he could make me a pair!

"Do you want ones with step-pads or trailer lights, or both?" Del asked. We settled on the step pads, and they arrived within a few weeks. Now I had the correct fenders on my newly painted yellow trailer. Another mission accomplished.

As I said earlier, my boat did not come with any motor, but that was not a problem for me. I had spent the winter restoring a 1952 twenty-five-horsepower Johnson outboard, along with a matching 1952 5½-horsepower Johnson kicker motor in anticipation of putting them on my future vintage boat.

These were totally restored right down to new paint and decals. One thing troubled me, about the twenty-five horse. It had a funny round protrusion connected to the throttle mechanism, sticking out of one side of the cowl. I could find no way to connect a remote throttle control cable to this. I couldn't find any information on this on the Internet. I even asked my good competitor, Joe, at Joe's Marine in Ely, if he knew what I needed. He'd been around Johnson outboards for fifty years and even he didn't know. I went back to my shop and walked up to look at it again, when I heard a car drive up. The car was trailering a

Above: Both tanks were cleaned, painted and decaled.

Left: Evinrudes ready to go!

vintage Crestliner with a vintage Gale outboard on it. Out comes a good friend and outboard collector, Dave Eveleth, from DesMoines, Iowa. He was up for a stay at his cabin and just wanted to say hi. He was always on the lookout for old outboards, and the previous summer I sold him a 1957 thirty-horsepower Evinrude. I asked him to look at the setup on my Johnson. Perhaps he'd know what I needed to do. "Oh, no, you won't find anything to hook up a remote on a '52," he told me. "You have to go to a '54 and later to do that."

The twenty-five would be useless to me then, because I wanted to get a boat with remote steering and controls. He said he'd be interested in buying it. **Coincidence number Six:** Just then, my dog, Cedar, started barking at something outside. When I looked out to see what it was, I saw Dave's van with the tailgate open and something blue-and-white lying there. I asked him if that was my thirty horsepower Evinrude that I had sold him. He said it was and that he brought it up as a standby motor in case his Gale broke down. So I did a couple quick calculation and said to him, "You said you were interested in my Johnson. Since my Johnson is worth more than the Evinrude in restored condition, how 'bout I trade you the Johnson for the Evinrude plus a matching '57 7-1/12 kicker motor?"

He said he had a great running 1957 kicker motor and that he'd bring it up in a few weeks. Bingo again! Problem solved!

During the boat restoration process, I also had both Evinrudes to restore. Both were sound, but I installed new points and condensers, impeller, carb cleanouts, and new plugs. I also painted both and added new decals. I restored both gas tanks as well.

By now the boat had been polished, painted and was sitting on the Tee Nee trailer. I now needed to start working on the wood seats and dash, and if I could find the money, get a new top made for it. **Coincidence number seven:** Each day, I parked the boat out front on the boulevard along our busy highway 169. Over 700,000 visitors passed by my shop each year on the way to Ely, a destination location, and to the Boundary Waters. One day I looked out the window and saw a man standing by the boat ogling it. By now it was getting all kinds of attention, as all old boats seemed to do. So I walked out to see if he had any questions. He said, "Wow, this is a beautiful old boat . . . and I like old things!"

I said, "If you like old things, you should come up to my shop and look at all the old vintage chain saws that I have on display."

He walked in and immediately asked if any of them were for sale. I assured him that EVERYTHING was for sale! He asked how much. I said that the ones that ran were $300, and the ones just cosmetically restored were $200. He asked me if he could get one price if he bought several. I agreed to $200 apiece. So he looked out the window and said, "Well, I have the small car today and can't take them, but give me that roll of green tape and I'll mark off the ones I want. I'll pay you now and pick them up later." He proceeded to mark off sixteen chainsaws! $3,200! I immediately had the top money made!

Things were really beginning to come together for me on this restoration. Unbelievably so. But now, I had to replace all the wood seats and the wood dash. My woodworking skills and tools were minimal, and I wasn't looking forward to paying out all the cash for tools and materials.

Coincidence number eight: I was mulling this over one day when a young gentleman I had helped get a new caretaking job came in to report how excited he was with his new career. I asked him what it was he had to do. He said the owners of the place wanted a complete restoration and that the place was huge. I asked what it involved, and he said, "I have to replace all kinds of woodwork. The place is so big I could have a permanent job! I asked if he had the tools to do the job, and he said, "I share a wood working shop in Ely, and we have every woodworking tool you can imagine." I showed him my boat and the woodwork I needed done and asked him if he could do it. "Not only can I do it, I'll do it all for free because you got me the best job I've ever had." Bingo, Bingo, Bango!

Beautiful oak dash built by August Cedergren.

Now for the final **coincidence, number nine!** This one almost gives me goose bumps when I think about it. Recently, I was able to track down the original owner of the boat. I asked for some history, and he said the boat spent many years first on Cass Lake, Minnesota. Cass Lake was where my father built our first cabin in 1957! I would have been a toddler then, but with so few cabins on the lake at that time it's very probable I waved at the people in the boat that would be mine . . . fifty-two years later!

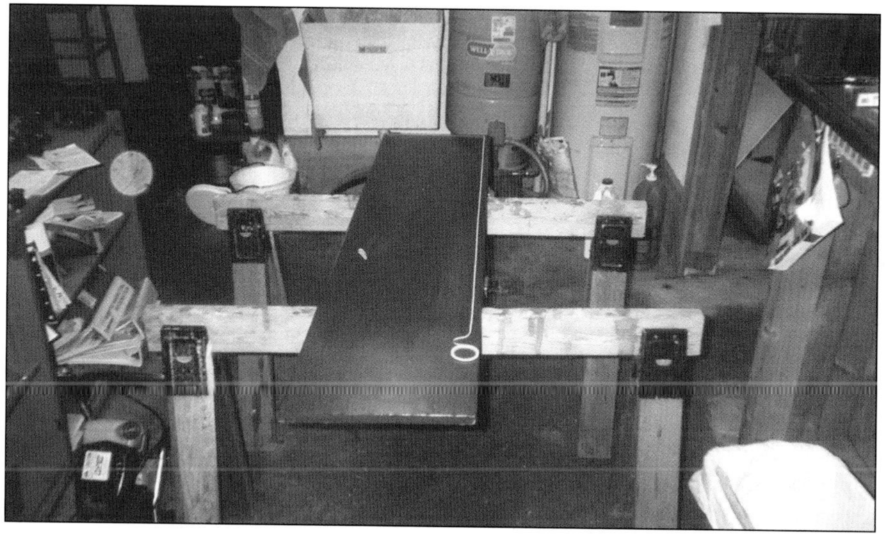

Bench seats are simple planking, chocolate brown with white pin stripping.

My brothers and I towheads looking out over Cass Lake, Minnesota ...We could be looking at my boat!

At the time of this writing, I have just completed all finishing touches on the boat. She saw her maiden voyage on beautiful Burntside Lake on Memorial Day 2009, exactly one year to the day after obtaining her! And I have just returned from her first succesfaul trip to the island in Canada. It will also be parked in front of my shop for all to see, as well as appear in parades, boat shows, and car shows. As former executive director of the North American Bear Center in Ely, my license plate reads Bear One. I have named my boat, Bear Two. If you ever get to Ely, stop out and see her!

Bear II

At speed on a beautiful day!

Boat, Family Reunited after More Than Fifty Years

By Jan Stadtherr

(Reprinted by permission of *Senior Perspective Magazine*)

A LOVE AFFAIR HAS BEEN REKINDLED for Ed Sheldon—an affair with a boat that is.

After over fifty years, the sixteen-foot Noeske wood speed boat, purchased by Ed's brother in 1955, has found its way back to the Sheldon family. Ed is now restoring the boat and estimates that 2,000 hours will have been spent on the classic boat before it is finally launched.

It was just by chance that Ed, who lives near Cold Spring, Minnesota, came upon the boat advertised for sale just a few miles from where he lived. "I remember when I was a kid, I would drool over the fancy wood boats on Fish Hook Lake (near Park Rapids), where we had the family cabin," Ed recalled. "I've loved wooden boats ever since!"

Ed's brother, Dave bought the Noeske boat in 1955, which was made by the Noeske Boat Works in Osage, Minnesota. Dave owned it, but Dad maintained it and the entire family used it," Ed remembered, as he pointed to various pictures of the boat pulling water skiers. "We fished from it and did a lot of water-skiing, too. My six daughters learned to ski from behind it. We had many good times with that boat!

Ed's brother, Don, in the 1950s.

Getting ready to go waterskiing!

Noeske Boat at speed.

As the owner of a classic 1950 Chris Craft purchased in 2001, Ed was looking for more wooden boats to purchase. In 2003, the daughter of his girlfriend, Bev, told him she saw a sign near Cold Spring that advertised an antique boat for sale. Ed went to look at the boat, took pictures of it and sent them to his brother, Lee, who lived in Eagan, Minnesota. Lee called Ed to say it looked like the boat their brother Dave had bought over fifty years ago.

To verify if it was the exact boat, Lee told Ed to look for a small block of wood on top of the deck that their father had mounted to hold a rear view mirror in order to see the water skiers behind. The block of wood was there.

Lee also asked if there was a small wooden shim behind the steering wheel that their dad had installed in order to angle the steering wheel, and that, too, was there!, said Ed. "It gave me goose bumps to know that this had been our boat!"

In retracing the boat's whereabouts, Ed explained that his brother had sold the boat to a distant relative thirty years ago. The relative moved to California and sold it to a step-grandson who was going to St. Cloud State University. His family kept the boat on Long Lake near Park Rapids. When he wanted to sell the boat, he erected a small sign by his driveway near Cold Spring.

"Dave paid $500 for the boat over fifty years ago, and I paid $1,000 for it," said Ed, "but the story is worth more than the value."

In restoring the boat, Ed had to remove many coats of paint his father had put on through the twenty years of ownership. He repaired the leaks and fiber glassed the bottom and then covered the fiberglass with epoxy before painting the bottom to its original dark green.

In researching the Noeske Boat Works, Ed found an article printed in the *Park Rapids Enterprise* newspaper in August 1953, which said that Charles Noeske had been building the quality cedar-strip row boats, fishing and speed boats since 1932. The company built about eighty boats per year ranging from twelve to sixteen feet in length. Cedar was shipped in from the West Coats. Philippine mahogany was used for the transoms and white oak for the framework. The boats were sold direct from the company, not through distributors.

Ed was also able to locate Melvin, the son of Charles Noeske, who believes that Sheldon's boat may be the last Noeske boat in existence.

"Wood boats deteriorate, and we just didn't think the old boat was around anymore," said Ed.

He pointed out the fine craftsmanship put into the boat by Noeske. The bottom is made of cedar. White oak strips were steamed in order to be pliable and were bent to line the inside of the boat.

"The strips were nailed on the outside and then clinched by another man in the inside. The making of these boats was labor intense," Ed noted. Copper nails were used in the top half of the boat.

The Sheldon family will gather on Fish Lake in August for the launching. A twenty-five-horsepower Johnson outboard motor will be used, a motor similar to the one the family used fifty years ago. But once the Noeske boat is afloat, Ed will continue his avid interest in restoring other boats.

Last August, Ed bought a 1957 Skee-Craft wooden speed boat made by the Amish in Pennsylvania. "There are four known boats of this type left in the world, so I just couldn't pass it up. It's heavy and built like a barn," he said as he knocked on the deep hull. His 1950 Chris Craft inboard, named *Ruby*, has won awards at classic boat shows. Ed purchased the boat in Texas and was pulling it back to Minnesota on September 11, 2001, the day terrorists struck the World Trade Center in New York City.

"I remember that day well as two of my daughters were flight attendants, so I had to check to see that they were okay, and they were," Ed recalled.

Besides restoring boats, Ed has also built two boats including a radio-controlled, scale model Chris Craft, appropriately named *Ruby 11*.

But his greatest pride is a fourteen-foot replica of a late 1920s Gentleman Racer, *Li'l Red*. "I've always loved wooden boats, but I've learned the most about them by building one," he said. "Building a boat is actually less work than restoring one." He ordered the plans for the boat from a company in Maine in 2002. "I bought a lot of mahogany and started making sawdust," he laughed. A party to launch *Li'l Red* was held ten months later. Ed claims the uniquely designed craft can skim over the water, up to forty miles per hour.

Ed has lived in the St. Cloud area for many years where he owned a construction management business, building apartments, fast-food restaurants and other commercial property. "I never drove a nail during all those years," he chuckled. "I was on the paper-end of the business. And now that I'm retired, I'm doing just the opposite, but I love it. I have every day to work on boats if I want." But he also finds time to do downhill skiing in the winter, fishing in the summer, bringing his boats to classic boat shows and, of course, the never-ending yard work around their home on Goodners Lake east of Cold Spring. Together, he and Bev have thirteen grandchildren.

Besides enjoying the nostalgia of the good times he and family members had with the old Noeske boat during the 1950s, the finding of the classic craft has brought he and his brothers closer together. "We talk a lot more now than we have in many years, and it's because the old boat has been found, and that's good. It will be a great get-together in August when we re-launch it!"

A follow up by the author—

Over one hundred friends and relatives turned out recently to watch as the old Noeske boat was re-launched. For a great video of the event, go to www.kare11.com, type in Ed Sheldon in search, and click on the video! The boat is on temporary display at the Minnesota Lakes Maritime Museum.

Ed takes the wheel . . . again!

Friends gather on launch day.

Ed planes her out!.

Chief Waramaug

By Ted and Barbara Grulikowski

An open door on one of Mertaugh Marine's storage buildings in Hessel, Michigan, seemed to be an invitation to go inside and look around. The opportunity that day in August 1997 was even more appealing because Mertaugh Marine was widely known throughout the U.S. as a source of rare Chris Craft boats and parts. Their reputation goes back to 1925 when they became Chris Craft's first franchised dealer. Who knew what was hiding behind those doors at Mertaugh's?

Looking around inside the storage building, my friend Chip DeBoer and I saw a few well-preserved triples, an old launch against the back wall and the front end of a dusty old wood boat sitting in the far rear corner. It was barely visible and surrounded by a white lapstrake and an unrestored Chris Craft utility.

What was amazing to us about this dusty old wood boat was how complete it looked. We climbed on a bench and got inside to inspect it. Everything that probably could have been ordered originally for this boat was still there, including cleats, instruments, gauges, windshield, rubber step pads, pike pole, paddle, walnut steering wheel, controls, mounted fire extinguisher, seat cushions, and upholstery. Only the stern pole and gas cap were missing. Looking further in and around the boat we found it even had a complete engine (old and neglected) as well as transmission, prop shaft, strut, propeller, and rudder. We had discovered an original unrestored diamond in the rough!

At that time, my wife, Barbara, and I had just purchased our second Grand Craft and hadn't thought much about buying a very old wood boat. But over the next few years the idea of owning and restoring a treasure like the one we found in storage at Mertaugh's became irresistible.

We feel very fortunate that we were able to acquire this boat in October 2000. By then we had figured out that the dusty old relic was in fact, a virtually complete 1927 Chris Craft Cadet, hull number 1028. Based on our research, the Cadet line of Chris Crafts was first introduced in 1927. One authority reported that during this period, Chris Craft hull numbers began at 1000, which would make this boat the twenty-eighth Cadet produced since introduction. Now that we knew what kind of boat we had, our attention turned to the engine.

Not knowing much about old marine engines, we had no idea what we were looking at when we saw the engine in this Cadet. With the help of a flashlight we could see there were no extra holes in the engine stringers, a good clue that this was the

original engine. After taking numerous pictures of the engine, we began asking wooden boating friends what they thought.

Numerous discussions followed and finally, at the Antique and Classic Boat Society (ACBS) annual meeting in September 2000, we discovered that the engine was a Scripps F6 Junior Gold Cup. Further conversation with Robert Henkel confirmed that the serial number was indeed a Scripps F6 Junior Gold Cup engine, shipped from Scripps Engine Co to Chris Smith and Sons Boat Co. May 5, 1927. Robert's father, Pete, acquired a copy of the original Scripps engine production history that is kept at the Mariners Museum.

Since winter was approaching and we had no immediate plans for the boat, we left it stored at Mertaugh's. In the meantime, we started on the journey of documenting the history of this beautiful, but seriously neglected, Cadet and figuring out how to restore it.

We had two clues that would lead us seventy-four years back in time. One was the name of the boat, still visible and painted on the sides forward of the windshield "Chief Waramaug." The second was a mention by the prior owner that it was purchased about twenty years ago from an acquaintance who wanted it out of a building on his property in Connecticut.

Working on the Internet and searching for the name "Waramaug," we discovered a lake in Connecticut named Lake Waramaug. Further searching uncovered an Indian chief named Waramaug. The excitement was boiling about then and work intensified to find people who knew about our boat. Numerous phone calls, letters, referrals, readings, and Internet searches were done. We even placed an ad in a Connecticut newspaper, which reached a man very knowledgeable of the boat. All of this led to a three-day research trip to Connecticut in August 2001 and shortly thereafter to a conversation directly with the son of the boat's original owner. The following is the history of our boat *Chief Waramaug*:

In January 1927, Mr. Stuart Mead of Greenwich Connecticut attended the New York Motor Boat Show held at the Grand Central Palace, New York City. There he met Christopher Columbus Smith and purchased one of the newly introduced Chris Craft Cadets from Chris Smith and Sons Boat Company, Algonac, Michigan. A copy of the original hull card shows a May 6, 1927, production date for Mr. Mead's hull #1028. Optional equipment included the Scripps engine and tools, straight front seat with removable center, full cover, and special flag.

Mr. Mead named his Cadet *Chief Waramaug* in memory of a highly regarded Connecticut Indian chief who died in 1735. Waramaug was the chief of an alliance of small local tribes in western Connecticut (the Pomperaugs, Bantams, Schaghticokes, Weatauges, Weantinokes, and Potatucks). These tribes banded together for protection from the Mohawks. Chief Waramaug had a reputation as a wise and able chief with great abilities and eminent virtues.

"Waramaug," means "place of good fishing." The second largest natural lake in Connecticut was in the chief's region and one of his favorite hunting and fishing grounds. This lake eventually became known as Lake Waramaug. The Mead family vacationed on Lake Waramaug for many years and owned a home and boathouse on the lake next to where the Boulders Inn stands today.

In the late 1920s and early 1930s, speedboats became all the rage on Lake Waramaug according to Mary Harwood, author of *History of Lake Waramaug*. This was also the time when large motorboats such as the Chris Crafts, including *Chief Waramaug*, arrived on the lake. As Mary described it, rivalries developed and calls of, "My Chris Craft is faster than your Chris Craft," led to many speedboat races.

Stuart Mead outfitted his Chris Craft Cadet with the 127-horsepower Scripps F6 Junior Gold Cup engine to help assure he would win over the Chrysler and Kermath powered boats of

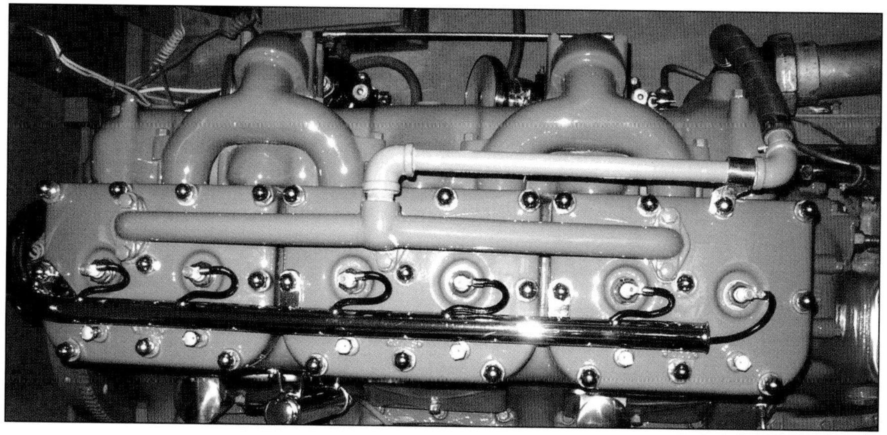

the day, particularly those belonging to George Blackiston and a Mr. Mulvahill, his key rivals. Although results were not kept back then, no doubt *Chief Waramaug* won its share of speedboat races over the years. Research has confirmed that Scripps produced 361 F6 Junior Gold Cup engines during the 1925–1930 period. Hacker purchased 163, Chris Craft 19 and the remainder were sold to numerous other boat builders.

The *Chief* continued to be used periodically by the Mead family on Lake Waramaug until the start of World War II. From that point forward it was rarely used. It hung in the Mead Boathouse on Lake Waramaug from 1927 until the Mead family sold it in 1979 to the Noyes family, who summered in Cedarville Michigan. The Noyes placed *Chief Waramaug* in storage until it was sold to us in October 2000.

Once we learned the history of *Chief Waramaug* we began to plan the boat's restoration. Being active members of the Michigan and Water Wonderland ACBS Chapters since 1990, we had already attended numerous wooden boat shows throughout the eastern half of the US and Canada with our Grand Crafts and had developed many friendships with wooden boat owners and restorers. One restorer, Russ Arrand, and his Cadillac Boat Company stood out as having all the qualities we wanted in our restorer: honesty, superior reputation and workmanship (as evidenced by his numerous first place restoration awards), good value and a keen personal interest in our project. Russ agreed to do the boat restoration and we couldn't have been happier. The only remaining question was, who would do the engine?

Scripps Junior Gold Cup engines are very rare today. Come to find out very few people know they even exist and even fewer own restored models.

In doing research on the Cadet and Scripps engine at Dick Sligh's Grand Craft Company (Dick has an incredible collection of old wooden boat magazines), we found the following article in the April 10, 1927 edition of *Motor Boat*: Two orders for Chris-Craft Cadets have recently been placed by T.E. Mitten and his son, Dr. A.A. Mitten of Philadelphia. Both boats will be driven by six-cylinder Junior Gold Cup Scripps motors, which will give them close to thirty-five miles per hour. They have identical equipment throughout and will be used on Long Lake.

We didn't know if the Mitten's still owned their Scripps Junior Gold Cup equipped Cadets, but we did discover in reading the ACBS Directory that two Hackers were registered as having Junior Gold Cup engines. After a few letters and phone calls we made contact with Les Rue, owner of the two Hackers. Les was most gracious and gave us his experience with the Scripps Junior Gold Cup engines. He suggested that George Shinn was best equipped to handle our engine restoration as he had already restored a number of Scripps Junior Gold Cup engines and that these engines were still running very well. A few conversations with George and some pictures of Scripps Junior Gold Cup engines he had restored convinced us that he was most qualified and we agreed that he would handle our engine restoration.

The restoration of *Chief Waramaug* began in June 2001 and was completed in June 2003. *Chief Waramaug* is now the only known operational Scripps F6 Junior Gold Cup equipped Chris Craft in existence.

P.S. *Chief Waramaug* returned to Lake Waramaug June 22, 2004, for a reunion with the lake (having been gone since 1979), the original owner's son (John Mead), and lake residents who remember the *Chief* as children living and playing on Lake Waramaug. At that reunion one of the only two missing hardware pieces—the original Stern Pole—was returned to the boat by John Mead whose family kept it since 1927 when John's father Stuart Mead purchased the boat from Chris Smith.

CHRIS CRAFT CADET

Chris Smith and Sons Boat Company introduced the "Cadet" at the New York Motor Boat Show January 21-29, 1927.

According to Dr. Thomas E. Jarrett, author of numerous boating articles, the origin of the word "Cadet" is unknown but may well have been the brainchild of A.W. "Bill" MacKerer, a well-known naval architect and design chief at Chris Craft. It was the first time a production boat had been given a special name ("Cadet") by the builders in Algonac, Michigan, where all the Cadets were built during the period 1927–1929.

The Cadet was advertised as a duplicate of the famous twenty-six-foot Chris Craft, but smaller for greater usefulness. Specifications included:

Length:	22 feet
Beam:	6 feet
Draft:	22 inches
Freeboard:	29 inches forward, 18inches aft
Construction:	All Mahogany
Bottom:	5/8 inch double planked
Sides:	1/2 inch
Speed:	25 - 35 mph
Motor:	Kermath (70 hp)
	Chrysler (82 -106 hp)
	Scripps (100 - 127 hp)
Fuel Capacity:	33 gallons
Net Weight:	2,805 lbs
Price:	$2,395 f.o.b. Algonac

Chris Craft planned to produce 500 Cadets during the 1927-1929 period. Only eighteen of the 1927 model Cadet are registered in the International Antique and Classic Boat Society Directory.

SCRIPPS F-6 JUNIOR GOLD CUP ENGINE

The following information is taken from the Scripps Motor Company, Detroit Michigan, Engine Catalog - 1927.

Scripps Motor Company introduced the Model F-6 engine in 1924 after the sensational success of the Model F-4 due to a demand for a larger size motor. "Lady Helen" was the first boat to carry a Model F-6 and made its first appearance by winning the Junior Gold Cup race at the Detroit Regatta on August 29, 1924. It was built by the Hacker Boat Company for Mr. Aaron DeRoy of Detroit. This international event was restricted to bonafide runabouts powered with motors not to exceed 335 cubic inches. The Scripps F-6 has a displacement of 331 cubic inches with power rated at 106 H.P. @ 2600 R.P.M.

Although the power output of the regular Model F-6 had not been approached for its displacement by any other manufacturer in the marine field, Scripps engineers, through a special development, materially increased the power of this wonderful engine for high-speed work and called the new application the Scripps F-6 Junior Gold Cup engine. In all major parts, the Junior Gold Cup engine is identical with the standard F-6, the modifications coming from refinements principally in the design of the cylinder heads, the manifolding, and the addition of dual carburetors. The Scripps F-6 Junior Gold Cup engine has a displacement of 331 cubic inches with power rated at 127 H.P. @ 2600 R.P.M.

The Scripps F-6 Junior Gold Cup engine has the same piston displacement as the regular machine, which makes it eligible for the Junior Gold Cup Class, the limit of which is 335 cubic inches. For racing it is likewise eligible for the 340-cubic-inch class in the Mississippi Valley Power Boat Association. The championships in this class as well as the Junior Gold Cup Class were won by the standard F-6.

Those who have followed racing and have had particular experience with the best developments in motors of every type were simply amazed at the perfect performance of this engine in the regattas held in Miami, Tampa, West Palm Beach, Jacksonville, and other Florida points. The Biscayne Baybies, built by Purdy, and the Tampa Baybies, produced by Hacker, both carry this model as stock equipment.

SPECIFICATIONS:
Motor - 6 cylinder, 4-cycle, bore 3, stroke 5"
Weight 750 lbs.
Power Developed - 127 H.P.@2600 R.P.M.
Price - $1350 f.o.b. Detroit

Few Scripps F6 Junior Gold Cup engines exist. Only four are registered in the International Antique and Classic Boat Society Directory.

Ted Grulikowski at the wheel!

The Thunderbird

Contributed by the Thunderbird Preservation Society
Photos by Dewitt Jones

GEORGE WHITTELL HAD A LIFELONG fascination with the latest technology of the day, particularly that which manifested itself in aircraft, automobiles, and boats. Among the many he owned were a Douglas DC-2 airliner, outfitted in luxury for his private use; a Grumman Goose amphibious airplane, five of the most uncommon Duesenberg motorcars, a 145-foot pleasure yacht named *Elia*, and the legendary fifty-five-foot speedboat, *Thunderbird*. The latter is certainly one of the most unique and elegant wooden vessels crafted in the twentieth century and is as much a work of art as a means of transportation.

Commissioned by Whittell specifically for Lake Tahoe while he was building his fabulous estate there, the *Thunderbird* was designed by famed naval architect John L. Hacker and built by Huskin Boat and Motor Works in Bay City, Michigan. Enamored by the art-deco styling of the era, it is said that Whittell asked Hacker to incorporate the lines of his DC-2—also named *Thunderbird*—and Duesenbergs. Fashioned of double-planked mahogany and having brushed stainless steel cabins, the new acquisition enabled Whittell to get about Lake Tahoe with unmatched style and speed. Originally outfitted with twin 550-horsepower Kermath V-

12 Sea-Raider engines, the vessel could cruise at more than fifty knots. To accommodate the *Thunderbird* its notoriously reclusive owner ordered the construction of a 100-foot long enclosed boathouse with 600-foot tunnel that would connect it to the main residence, both blasted out of solid granite.

Shipped by rail and completed at a cost of $87,000 (over $3.3 million in today's dollars), Whittell took delivery of *Thunderbird* at Mayfield's (Tahoe City Marina) in 1940. For the first time that year, she crossed the lake to her new home in the pre-dawn hours of July 14th. The aging sportsman cruised extensively that summer and the next, shuttling friends and supplies from nearby communities and showgirls from the Cal-Neva casino for lavish parties at his estate. Following the U.S. entry into World War II, possibly afraid his beloved yacht or its engines might be conscripted into military service, Whittell hid her away in lodge's boathouse.

Whittell became even more reclusive as he entered his seventies. His yacht was seen so infrequently that it seemed to some who caught a glimpse to be nothing more than an apparition.

When Whittell broke his hip late in life and refused surgery to repair the fracture, he was confined to a wheelchair and unable or unwilling to use *Thunderbird*. Resting idly in the boathouse for many years, *Thunderbird* was rescued by casino magnate and car collector William F. Harrah who purchased her from Whittell in 1962 along with two Duesenberg autos. Harrah rotated the vessel between his Skyland, Lake Tahoe villa; restoration shops in Sparks, Nevada; and winter storage at the Whittell boathouse. Harrah's workmen added a matching stainless steel superstructure and replaced the original Kermath engines with vintage World War II fighter aircraft engines: these V-12 Allison V-1710 motors develop 1,100 horsepower each. Harrah called *Thunderbird* his "seventy-mile-per-hour cocktail lounge" and frequently entertained showroom headliners aboard including Tony Bennett, Sammy Davis, Jr., Liberace, and Bill Cosby, to name a few. Harrah was meticulous and, each year, his team sanded down the wooden hull and applied ten new coats of varnish!

Thunderbird is now owned by Foundation 36, a Nevada public charity founded by casino entrepreneur Bill Watson for the purpose of saving Nevada's historic and cultural treasures. Tahoe's most famous yacht still operates and serves as a cruising classroom to educate the public about Lake Tahoe's rich maritime heritage and fragile marine environment. When she is in port, Thunderbird resides in her original boathouse and may be viewed as visitors tour the Thunderbird Lodge estate.

For information on the Thunderbird Lodge estate, visit wwwThunderbird Lodge.org.

Memories of a Lady

By Chip DeBoer

EVERY BOAT HAS A HISTORY and a story to tell, but all too often those tales are lost to time and circumstances beyond our control. I'm fortunate to have had the opportunity to rediscover the detailed history of our boat and the chance to share her story.

Lady Phyllis II is a 1938, nineteen-foot, split cockpit runabout that was built for my grandfather, Angelo Givone, at the Greenwood Lake Launch Works in Sterling Forest, New York.

My initial exposure to the world of antique and classic boating began with a phone call from New Jersey to my home in Kalamazoo, Michigan, one cold night in February 1989. It was my aunt, Phyllis Givone Ryan, saying, "The boat in the boathouse is causing the roof to sag," and she didn't know what to do.

My first question to her was, "What boat?" I was both shocked and pleasantly surprised when she replied, "Grandpa's boat, *Lady Phyllis II*." It had been years since I had even thought of that the old boat hanging in the boathouse.

Asking her what she wanted to do she said, "Sell it, I guess."

Flashback recollections of the boat went through my mind, but I must admit I had to shake a few cobwebbed memories loose. I had become a Michigan resident since leaving New Jersey in 1963 to attend college. And though I returned frequently for visits with my parents and other relatives, I never gave much thought to the lake property or what might eventually happen to the boat.

My grandfather was very protective of his boat, and it was a rare occasion for it to be used or even in the water in the

years following World War II. To us kids, it was just an old boat hanging in the boathouse. It had always been "off limits" to my cousins and me when we visited the lake. We lived under the constant warning to, "Stay out of the boathouse and away from the mahogany boat."

The only childhood recollection I have of actually being in the boat while it was in operation on the lake occurred when I was about five years old (circa 1950). I distinctly remember the roar of the engine, going fast, hitting a big wave, getting soaking wet in the aft cockpit and being "passed" forward by my uncle over the engine hatches to the forward cockpit.

My father, a man who could not swim a stroke and almost drowned when he was a boy, witnessed this event from shore, and I believe this was the last time I was allowed to go out in that boat! Of course, being kids, we only considered the warnings about staying away from the boat to be a challenge to our ingenuity. We would sneak down to the water's edge, swim under the boathouse door and play in and on the boat as it hung from its lifts.

Angelo Givone was a loving and giving grandfather but he was also a believer in natural consequences for bad behavior. He could become a very firm disciplinarian if provoked. None of us wanted to provoke him so secrecy in these adventures was of utmost importance.

One day, when I was about eleven, my cousin and I snuck into the boathouse. While kneeling on the deck of the boat, I accidentally cracked the glass in the folded-down windshield. I think I lived in fear of my cousin spilling the beans and my grandfather finding out about the damage right up until his passing in 1968!

At the time of the original phone call all I knew about wooden boats was that they were made of wood. But I assured

Aunt Phyllis that I'd do some research on the wooden boat market to help her sell the boat when I came out to assess the situation in the spring.

April of 1989 arrived and my youngest son, Matthew, and I made the 700-mile trip to New Jersey. Arriving at the boathouse we entered and made our way through years of cobwebs. To get to the boat we had to remove no less than twenty-five years worth of dust, swallow droppings, eight automobile tires, two aluminum folding tables, six layers of miscellaneous sheets, bedspreads, table cloths, and one original but very deteriorated canvas mooring cover "protecting" the boat. After clearing the decks, we were amazed at the relatively good condition of the wood and varnish. Even the deck seams were reasonably tight. We took a wet towel and after one swipe the deck looked almost brand new! Except for being dark, the varnish even looked fresh.

Further inspection was done, and we found that all of the original hardware and gauges were intact. She had a Gray Marine Fireball 6-160 engine complete with the original Scintilla magneto triple carburetors mounted in a triangular "tarantula" configuration. The only item missing was her stern pole, which, according to my aunt, was eaten by a porcupine many years ago.

The damage to the boathouse was caused by one cracked support beam, which allowed the weight of the boat to pull on the attached lifting winches. We easily repaired the beam and this might have been the end of this story but Aunt Phyllis said she still wanted to sell the boat.

My son and I took lots of pictures and returned to Michigan to continue our research. Numerous phone calls and many contacts with restoration shops led us to Steve Northuis at Macatawa Bay Boat Works. He was very helpful in determining a value for the boat and the potential for selling it, as well as providing restoration information.

We shared our findings with Aunt Phyllis but she now seemed less enthusiastic about selling. After all, it had belonged to her father, and the boat had been named after her and she even had been the first passenger on the day they picked it up in 1938.

A few days later she called, saying she "could not stand the thought of selling Poppa's boat to a stranger," and, "what I would do if I were in her shoes." I said I would like to see her try and get the boat back into running condition and she replied, "I want you to do it—and I'm giving you the boat."

The rest is history. My wife and I became the owners of what turned out to be the most expensive "free" boat in history!

The boat was transported to Michigan in August of 1989. I got to the lake three days prior to the arrival of the folks that were going to pick up the boat. Plenty of time, I thought, to prepare it for the trip.

Lowering the boat into the water for the first time in twenty-six years was a real education. I couldn't believe the amount of water she rapidly took on! At some time in her neglected past, *Lady Phyllis* must have become a warehouse for a mouse or a squirrel. Hundreds of acorns came floating up as water quickly filled the bilge. If it had not been for the lifting lines she would have gone straight to the bottom. What was I thinking? Did I really expect the boat to float?

I made two sixty-mile round trips each day from my parents' home to the lake to bail the boat out. Each time I met with disappointment: the lift lines were found tight, the bilge full of water and water above the waterline. At least I was making progress on the acorns.

Arriving at the lake early in the morning of the third and final day I again expected the worst. Armed with a large plastic tarp to use as a "diaper" around the bottom of the boat I opened the boathouse door and was overjoyed to find *Lady Phyllis II*

proudly floating in the boat well with slack lift lines and very little water in her bilge!

The towboat arrived and Aunt Phyllis joined me in our boat for the trip across the lake, sitting in her favorite place on the engine hatch with her feet on the front seat. We attached a towline to the stern and began pulling the boat out for our journey across the lake. The overcast morning gave way to bright sunshine the minute the boat left the boat well as if to welcome her back to the world. Looking over at Aunt Phyllis, I saw that she was crying and asked her if she had changed her mind. "No, I'm just remembering all of the good times we had in this boat and how much it meant to Poppa. I'm looking forward to the time when she's up and running again."

Back in Michigan, Steve Northuis at Macatawa Bay Boat Works took over the restoration activities. Since the boat was in such good shape, her needs were expected to be—and remained—minimal: stripping and refinishing, rechroming and reupholstering. The Gray engine was to be rebuilt and gauges gone

through. We all looked forward to getting her back in the water again.

I began the task of researching the history of the boat, her manufacturer and her racing history. This task was not as easy as I thought it would be. Over time, people's memories had faded or become exaggerated. Also, almost all of the local libraries around the lake suffered fires or other disasters and historical records that might have been helpful had been lost.

One of the best moves I made was joining the Antique and Classic Boat Society. The ACBS Directory and Bob Speltz's books ,*The Real Runabouts*, really came through for me. They provided valuable initial information about the builders and helped me locate five other vintage Morin Craft owners. Eventually, I was able to get in touch with Mike Morin, Jr., the son of the builder.

In the early 1900s three brothers, Mike, Nick, and Otto Morin emigrated from Austria to the United States and settled in the Greenwood Lake area. The lake is located in northern New Jersey on the border of New York State. Since it is only about forty miles from New York City, Greenwood Lake has always been a popular destination for vacationers. The main method of travel to the lake in the earlier part of the last century was through northern Jersey by train. The rails ended at the New York/New Jersey border in the hamlet of Sterling Forest.

Arriving at their final destination, lake visitors soon realized that the only way to get to the many hotels, camps, cottages, and resorts located around the lake was by boat. Many entrepreneurs began to develop their own "fast" boat livery services for this captive audience.

The Morins' primary source of income came from working for the local ice house. During winter they would cut huge blocks of ice from the lake for storage in a large building on the shore of the lake.

Around 1912, they formed the Greenwood Lake Launch Works and began operation of a boat building, repair, and livery service that lasted into the 1950s. In the winter they built, sold, repaired and rented gaff rigged iceboats reported to be among the fastest on the lake. In the summer they did the same with small sail and pulling boats for their customers.

Under the leadership of Mike Morin, the Greenwood Lake Launch Works began building mahogany runabouts. Production records are non-existent but we speculate they only built two or three boats per year. These boats were usually preordered and custom built for their prospective owners, ranging in size from eighteen to thirty-two feet. They called their boats "MORIN CRAFT." The Morins weren't opposed to "borrowing" design features from other manufacturers and bits of Hacker, Chris-Craft and Gar Wood designs can be seen in their products. They were also "authorized agents" for Gar Wood boats so much of their hardware was of Gar Wood manufacture.

As we all know, once more than two powerboats arrive on a lake, speed and racing are soon to follow. Racing events became so popular that the Woodlands Hotel began sponsoring them. The Woodlands Boat and Country Club (WBCC) races were "free for all" events and open to all classes of boats. Over the years, Morin Craft boats developed a great racing history on the lake beating some of the biggest names in competition.

My grandfather got the racing bug and in 1937. He contracted to have the Morins build a runabout for him that would be a contender for the 1938 Greenwood Lake races. According

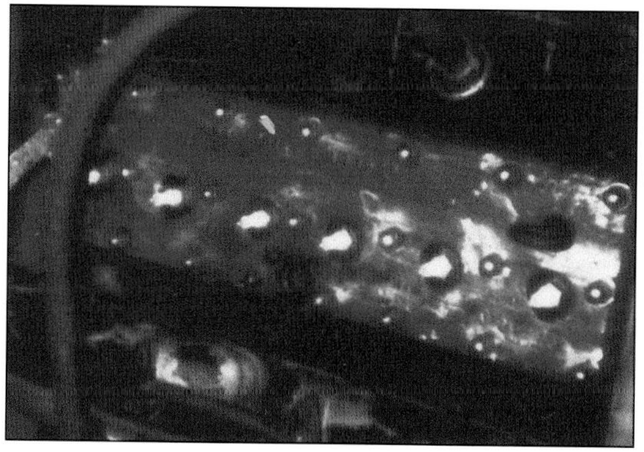

to family lore, Mike Morin "guaranteed" Angelo a boat that would have a winning racing season and the deal was sealed!

A contract dated February 11, 1938, called for the boat to be completed by May 28th at a cost of $1,375.00. The addition of

the Gray engine increased the total by another $350.00. Apparently my grandfather didn't like the cost of the original steering wheel and windshield so he "downgraded" to Gar Wood equipment and got a $55.50 credit. What a deal!

That year, *Lady Phyllis II* won all three of the major races sponsored by the WBCC! The three loving cups awarded for "Fastest Boat," "Championship of Greenwood Lake," and "Winner, Lake George Race" are proudly displayed at the boat shows we attend. We believe that a Lake George race was either a long distance or an endurance type of event since we know that our boat was never taken to Lake George.

Needless to say, the family was very proud of the boat's performance, and plans were made to "do it again" in 1939. I'm sure a lot of bragging occurred over that summer and the following winter months leading to the 1939 racing season.

According to family recollections, here's what allegedly happened during the races of 1939.

The marina where our boat was being readied for the racing season was supposed to tune the engine and remove the boat from the water for a week to let her dry out and lighten her before the big race. They didn't do this and the boat was much heavier than it should have been. Charges of intentional sabotage were launched! In spite of this weight disadvantage, my grandfather ran as many of the elimination heats as he could, but the boat just could not make enough speed and *Lady Phyllis II* didn't even place. There are reports of fists and wrenches flying following the last heat as my grandfather tried to make his point with those responsible.

Remember what I said about the Morins' "guaranteeing" that a boat that they built for a customer would be the fastest boat on the lake for the current racing season? The boat that won all of the races in 1939 was a brand new Morin Craft built for a customer from New York City.

Following the fiasco of 1939, *Lady Phyllis II* kept a very low profile on the lake. Angelo had lost his desire to race and only used the boat occasionally at relatively low speeds, just as my grandmother wished. During the war years the boat was not used much due to the shortage of fuel and rationing. I guess you could say that this was the beginning of her very long and lonely stay in a dark boathouse.

Restoration of *Lady Phyllis II* was completed in 1991. Except for new upholstery and a replaced vintage stern pole, all of the hardware, engine components, instruments, and wood were original. We attended four boat shows that summer and we were hooked after the first one! Over the next six years we traveled all over the country attending four or five boat shows each year making many new friends along the way. Wherever we went, *Lady Phyllis II* continued to be a crowd pleaser and remained a consistent award winner.

Aunt Phyllis traveled with us as often as possible and she became an expert at the art of eavesdropping. Sitting or standing in an inconspicuous place near the boat at a show, she really enjoyed listening in on the comments that spectators and judges would make about the boat. She was very proud of the boat and continually said how happy "Poppa" would be.

Unfortunately, Aunt Phyllis passed away in June 1997. She has been greatly missed. That year we only had the boat in the water once following her death. It just wasn't the same without her. We placed the boat in storage, and that's where she stayed for almost seven years.

In 2004 we felt it was time to get the boat back in operation. We decided that it would be fitting to bring the boat back to her home waters in New Jersey for a visit with the friends and family who had been so helpful to us in our efforts. Lake Hopatcong is only twenty-five miles from Greenwood Lake, and we attended Lake Hopatcong Chapter's thirtieth anniversary boat show before driving to our lake. *Lady Phyllis II* was warmly welcomed, and we had some great conversations with many of the locals who remembered the Morins and the races held in the past. We proudly accepted the First Place award presented for "Antique Runabout Under 20 Feet."

Following the boat show we traveled the short distance to Greenwood Lake. One of the biggest highlights of this nostalgic trip home was having the opportunity to finally meet Mike Morin, the son of the man who built our boat. He arrived lakeside with several of his children and a camera, only expecting to meet us and take a few pictures. His eyes got as big as saucers when I said, "Let's go for a boat ride." Needless to say, it didn't take too much convincing.

Mike got in the boat, two of his children got into the aft cockpit and off we went. He may not admit it, but I saw a few tears in his eyes as he turned to his children and said, "My dad's sweat is in the boards of this boat."

Many people over the past fifteen years have helped us with information, history, and the restoration of our boat. She is a memorial to people and times past as well as a memory maker for the future. *Lady Phyllis II* has been in our family since day one and will remain so with us as her stewards.

In 1992, my Aunt Lillian wrote me a letter. She had just seen a video that we'd sent her showing the first launching of the boat following her complete restoration. She wrote, "For a brief moment I was a happy twenty-five-year-old again, enjoying the race and tasting the delicious "Winners Cup" punch at the Woodland Hotel where the race was held. The family and the *Lady* have had a love affair of long standing and it is good to see her so beautiful again. When I saw how beautifully you had restored her, I could only think that Grandpa, wherever he

might be, must be very happy to know you thought so much of his pride and joy."

I'm sure that Aunt Phyllis would echo those statements.

Over time we've come to understand a little better my grandfather's love for this boat and his reasons for being so protective of her. If Gramps were here, I like to think he'd smile and say, "Well done! . . . and by the way, it's okay about that cracked windshield . . ."

Rumble

The Story of the Last Known Remaining Boat Designed by Virgil Exner!

By Bob Matson and Bill Fellner

In my introduction, I stated that I was a car enthusiast. So when I heard about a boat designed by a *car* guy, it really interested me. This is the story of the last remaining boat, designed by Virgil Exner . . . a 1966 Buehler, twenty-four-foot Bar Harbour turbocraft jetboat. The boat is owned by Bill Fellner of London, Ontario.

Famous for his automotive designs with Chrysler Corporation, Exner became interested in designing his own series of cabin cruisers. Because designing boats was so different from designing cars, Exner searched for help and found Bob Hobbs. Exner and Hobbs formed Exner-Hobbs & Associates and started to design boats. They read an article in *Popular Boating* that helped raise a lot of interest, so both Exner and Hobbs got in touch with Buehler Turbocraft of Indianapolis, Indiana, known for their jet-powered boats.

In 1962, several designs were suggested to Buehler, and in 1966, seven Bar Harbour boats were built. They were powered by a Chrysler marine 426 cubic-inch wedge V8, and coupled to a Hamilton three-stage jet pump. Notice the striking resemblance to the 1966 Dodge Charger, also designed by Exner.

Through the decade of the 1960s, Buehler had some exciting clientele. Among them was the secret service for the protection of the First Family. Jackie Kennedy owned a jet 35 for waterskiing. In video clips from the Kennedy Administration, you will see John John Kennedy sitting on the lap of President Kennedy behind the wheel of a Jet 35.

Another notable story that has been told is that of Nikita Kruschev. In the late summer of 1962 he ordered a Jet 35 and it was on the transport plane to the Soviet Union in October of 1962, when it was called back in midflight due to the Cuban Missle Crisis. In the 1965 James Bond movie *Thunderball*, a nineteen-foot Buehler Turbocraft was used for a cameo role of taking Commander James Bond back to shore with a beautiful woman (of course). Buehler quickly capitalized on this and aptly named the new nine-foot model *Thunderball*.

As the 1960s came to a close, the Buehler Turbocraft came upon hard times. When the Nixon presidency came into being, so did government cuts in defense spending. At this time the Marine Division of Indiana Gearworks (Buehler's parent company) was sold in an effort to save the core business of manufacturing precision gears for the aircraft industry. The Marine division was sold in May of 1971 and the last Turbocraft was produced. It was an end of an era!

Not much is known about what happened to the seven Bar Harbour boats, other than the fact that Bill Fellner's boat was originally imported into Canada for EXPO 67.

In 2005, Bill Fellner found pieces of a Bar Harbour boat lying in a junk boat yard. He has since undergone a complete "water" up restoration of the boat to original condition using the same colors in and out.

The following picture gallery tells the story of it's restoration. My credit goes to Bill for his exacting standards in bringing back another piece of nautical history!

Rumble was recently shown at the Toronto Antique and Classic Boat Show in Gravenhurst, Ontario. My thanks to Fibergalassic.com and to Royce A. Humphreys for further information on Buehler boats.

Author's note—At the time this went to press, another Bar Harbour boat had been found in Oregon!

290

The Holy Grail

By Bob Matson

OVER THE YEARS, one of the questions about old boats I would hear was, "Whatever happened to the boat used in the movie, *On Golden Pond*?" I heard this many times traveling to boat shows and I saw the question too, on boat blogs and Internet sites. I didn't know, or even hoped to find an answer up here at the end of the road, but then . . . it happened!

On December 23, 2008, an ad for a boat showed up on EBay, and it was advertised as *Thayer IV*, the boat used in the movie. The listing received over 12,000 page views and eventually was sold to a successful, but anonymous bidder. I tried to get information on the new owner through the previous owner, but to no avail. I also tried to get information from Pat Curtain, the marine coordinator on the movie, but after much debate, he reserved the right not to say anything at all until he could see the boat. This might have been the end of the story, but then it happened to me again! Provenance!

Two years later, I planned to travel down to the Bob Speltz Land O' Lakes Chapter Rendezvous Boat Show on Lake Minnetonka. I figured I had better get a motel room the night before so I could get to the show early with my Crestliner. I checked in, bought a newspaper and set it aside for later, went to dinner, then decided I would read the paper with my coffee in the morning. But at 3:00 a.m., something woke me. Not able to get back to sleep, I reached down to pick up the paper. I opened it to the local section, and there before my eyes was an article about the new owners of the *On Golden Pond* boat appearing the next day at the Rendezvous boat show with the newly restored boat! The owners' were Jeff and Nancy Thom, and they

were not only from Minnesota, they were from Mankato . . . my former town! Needless to say, I did not go back to sleep. I rehearsed how I was going to approach them a thousand times, to get their story. When the time came, I packed everything up and headed for the show.

After setting up my display, I headed for the docks to eagerly await the arrival of *Thayer IV* and the new owners. With heart pounding, I introduced myself and quickly inserted the fact that I too, was from Mankato. After a little bonding, they graciously offered to give me their story for this book. Now surely this should have been the end of the story, but it just gets more intriguing.

During this same time, I had several discussions with Matt Smith, the humorous owner of Woodyboater.com, the web site billed as the number one daily journal for antique and classic boat lovers. I told him I had the story of the *On Golden Pond* boat and I was writing a book about old boats. He quickly reminded me that he had been working on the same story for several years, and he was also working directly with Pat Curtain, the marine coordinator for the movie; "the only man who would know for sure" he said. He suggested another boat had been used in the movie and that I should look closely at Jeff Thom's boat. "Something about the steering wheel," he said. Several months went by and then on November 8, 2010, his story was released on Woodyboater's website. I include this story as well as Jeff Thom's story in the following two chapters and make no claim to which boat is the real *Thayer IV*, other than the fact that there were two boats used in the movie and that both are the real thing. I want to thank Jeff Thom, Matt Smith and Pat Curtain for bringing us their stories. Enjoy!

On display on Lake Minnetonka.

The Blessings of a "Golden" Opportunity

Submitted by Jeff and Cindy Thom

In the early 1980s, when I was around twenty years old, I worked with a gentleman who owned a wooden Chris Craft boat that was built in the early 1950s. After he restored it, he had named it after his wife, *Audrey LaVae*. I was at his house on the lake, one spring, when he put it in the water. To my amazement, when he backed the boat and trailer into the water, it stayed on the trailer and began filling up with water. He said that was all there was to it. He unhooked the trailer, told me to get into his pickup, and we drove back up the hill to his house. Once he explained the need to swell the wood each year, I better understood the process but not the logic. I remember thinking, *Why would anyone want a boat that doesn't float immediately, when you put it in the water?* I sure didn't get it, or even come close to understanding why anyone would go through the process of restoring an old boat that, when done, still didn't float.

Later that same year, I was fortunate to be offered a ride in that boat and then I understood. After only ever experiencing fiberglass boats, I remember enjoying the ride and thinking, *Now this is a boat!* After hearing the engine, feeling the ride and truly experiencing its beauty, I was sure I wanted to have one someday.

Approximately twenty-five years later, I came home from work one day and my wife, Cindy, said, "There's something in the newspaper I probably shouldn't show you." After twenty years of marriage and raising our sons Joseph and Andrew together, she knew me all too well. She knew I would need to see what she was talking about and if she didn't want me to, she wouldn't have brought it up.

I read the article and couldn't believe it. One of the boats used in the 1981 movie *On Golden Pond* was for sale and being

In the movie On Golden Pond.

At Sunrise Boat Works.

auctioned on E-bay. The article said that the seller had all of the documentation to prove its use in the movie. Since that movie was and is one of Cindy and my favorites, we were thrilled.

After some soul searching, and discussions with our sons about what exactly E-bay was, we decided to move forward and bid on the famous boat called the "Thayer IV" named after the main characters in the movie, Norman and Ethel Thayer. After discussions, Cindy and I agreed that this boat, a U22 Chris Craft Sportsman, was a collectible worth acquiring, restoring and taking care of.

Prior to us beginning the bidding process, the person who provided the boats used in the movie, a Mr. Pat Curtin, told the *Minneapolis Tribune* that there were a total of four U22's bought for the movie but only three received screen time. Our research had already shown us that there were rumors of many more as well. If we were the successful bidder of the E-bay boat, we would then need to authenticate that the boat was one of the boats Mr. Curtin had supplied and used in the movie. On January 1, 2009, we accomplished our initial goal of being the highest bidder on the E-bay auction.

I then spent about three weeks becoming somewhat of an archivist and when doing so, I found several things that verified the E-bay boat's use in the movie. First, there were several articles that confirmed Mr. Curtin provided the U22s, the mail boat, a canoe, and a small outboard fishing boat for the movie. They also confirmed that one of the U22s he provided was used as a replica of the *Thayer IV*, for the crash scene. We figured that if Mr. Curtin didn't know what happened to those boats, no one would. According to the *Laconia Evening Citizen*, picturing Mr. Curtin and the buyer shaking hands by the boat, Curtin sold the E-bay U22 and

'Golden Pond' Boat Headed For Key Largo

By MIKE MORTENSEN

Jim Hendricks admires the almost-glasslike finish on the hull of the 22-foot Chris-Craft runabout sitting on a trailer outside a boat-refinishing shop in Laconia. With a twinkle in his eye he tells a visitor, "There's going to be a new girl in town."

Hendricks, a retired lawyer from Louisville, Ky., is speaking affectionately about the Thayer IV — the boat that Henry Fonda and Katharine Hepburn navigated over Squam Lake in the Academy Award-winning movie "On Golden Pond."

Sometime in October, after all the refinishing work is complete, the 33-year-old craft will be hauled down to Key Largo, Fla., where it will become both Hendricks' personal boat and a tourist attraction.

There, in the island community which was the setting for one of Humphrey Bogart's famous films, Hendricks plans to display Thayer IV along

Movie Boat

Hendricks and Curtain shaking hands.

the crash boat, to Mr. Jim Hendricks of Largo, Florida, in the fall of 1983. The article confirmed this boat was "the boat which Henry Fonda and Katharine Hepburn used for their excursions on Golden Pond." With that information in mind, it was no problem to follow the ownership from the Hendricks family to the E-bay seller. Once I confirmed this was the boat Curtin sold to Hendricks, U22-1802, I then talked with Jim Hendricks, Jr., as he was there when his father took delivery from Mr. Curtin. He also knew specifics of the boat, as told to him and his father by Mr. Curtin, and he was around the boat for the twenty years his family had possession of it. He was kind enough to share the changes his family made during their ownership and sign an affidavit confirming the delivery of hull number U22-1802, from Mr. Curtin to his father. There were certain aesthetic differences when comparing the E-bay boat and the one in the movie, but Mr. Hendricks was able to explain, to my satisfaction, the changes that were made over the years and the reasons for them.

Since we had the aforementioned documentation proving the Hendricks U22 (1802) was used in the movie, we gladly moved forward and on the 22nd of January 2009, Cindy and I wrote a check to the seller for $47,000. We were now the proud owners of the *Thayer IV*, used in the movie, *On Golden Pond*.

I then began to research our restoration options only knowing that we wanted it to be restored in Minnesota, so we could learn about the process as we made restoration decisions. We knew we were looking at a fairly thorough restoration and wanted to be in close proximity to the restorer. After talking with several restorers, I was most comfortable with Tom Moravec of Sunrise River Boatworks, in Wyoming, Minnesota (since moved to Forest Lake, Minnesota). As this fine boat deserved, an excellent restoration was completed. These guys are truly artists.

After the restoration of the *Thayer IV*, we displayed her at the Bob Speltz Land O' Lakes Chapter of the Antique and Classic Boat Society's, thirty-fifth annual rendezvous. This boat's participation in the movie helped to generate an increased amount of interest in the restoration and care of antique wood boats. That is why we wanted to share it with our fellow wood boat enthusiasts and the public as well and why we feel it is an important piece of American culture. We feel truly blessed to be the proud stewards of this wonderful collectible and we intend on giving the *Thayer IV* the care it deserves.

Dark Side of the Pond

By Matt Smith
Photos by Frank Miklos

AS MANY JOURNEYS START, this one starts years before the journey actually happens. My journey regarding the *On Golden Pond* boats started in a rather undramatic way. On eBay . . . I suppose the Internet is doing that for many folks these days. I had seen images from a scrapbook on a boat forum regarding the shoot from the film *On Golden Pond*. I did not know more than that really . . . I knew of a guy in my home town who was claiming to have the boat. I did not think about it much. But when I saw the snap shots, it did make me think, *Hey, that's a U22, not a runabout like my neighbor . . .*

And then on December 23, 2008, the *On Golden Pond* boat, serial number 1802, came up for sale on eBay! Well, there you have it. I was bitten. I had to know more. As I dug into it, I found one simple thing . . . all *On Golden Pond* boats lead to one place . . . Pat Curtain. So I called him. WOW, what a great guy . . . and very helpful. Pat was the marine coordinator on the film and, in fact, one of Hollywood's golden boys when it came to that sort of thing. His film credits include *Striking Distance*, *Water World*, *Interview with a Vampire*, and of course *On Golden Pond*. One of the first things out of Pat's mouth was, "You know there are three of them." What? Three? One main picture boat, one stand by, and one wreck boat. Okay . . . which was which, and did it really even matter?

As it turned out, the boat on eBay was one of the three. Sold to a Jim Hendricks and carted around the US as the boat from the film. Mr. Hendricks also owned the crash boat and this boat was located in the Keys as an attraction. The third one, the main picture boat as it turns out, was sold with the US Mail boat *Mariah*, to a New England family. But there was no name given and it was thirty years ago. In the meantime, I was out-bid on the eBay boat now known as #1802 . . . way out bid! I thought at the time, *Well, that was fun and I would have loved to see 1802 one day*. And I moved on.

Until a year later. Number 1802 was restored and out there! What a wonderful restoration. The bug hit me again. I wanted to find the third boat. So I dug in. Pat and I went through papers, and we just talked, almost every day for a year. We knew the name of the buyer, of course, because Pat had sold them the boat. That was the easy part. Only no one by that last name in the US claimed the boat. Until one day. Then, one of the family members said, "Yes, the boats are still around, but not here." What? This is getting worse! So we kept chipping away. We

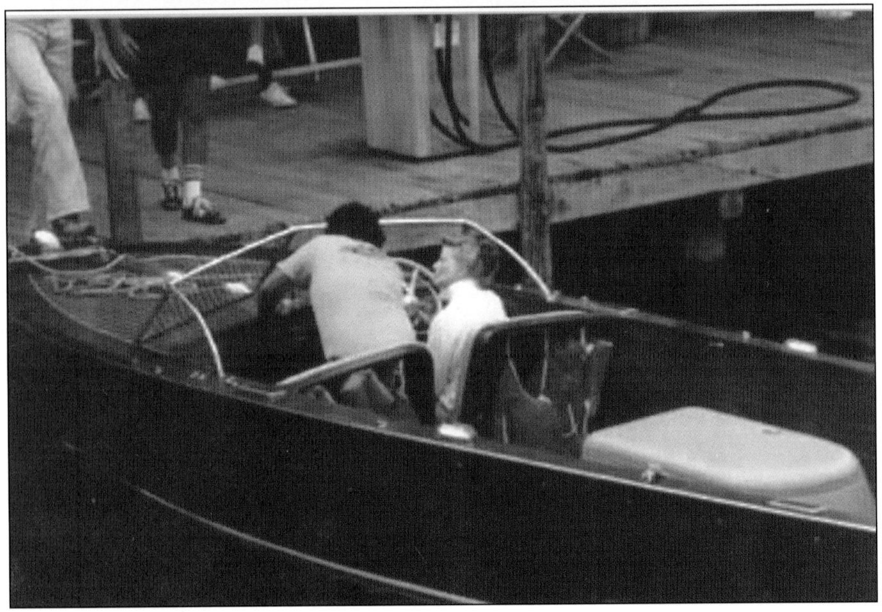

Boat supervisor Pat Curtin instructs Katherine Hepburn in the Cris Craft.

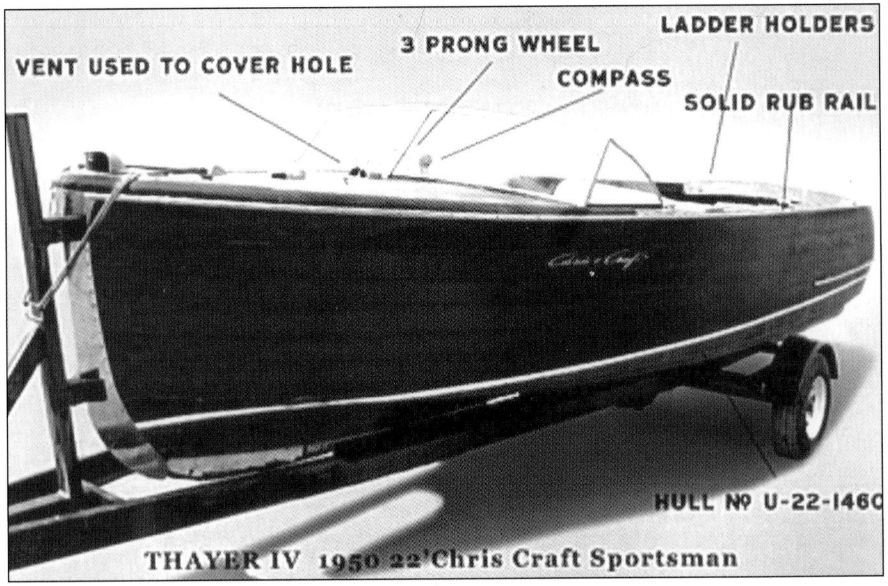

went through hang-ups and unanswered emails after another. Then we figured out that the boat had gone to the daughter of the buyer who had died three years after purchasing it, and she had her name changed by marriage. Bingo! But still no answered emails or phone calls.

Then one day in the office, a call comes in. Turns out the family is extremely private, and the boats have been in the family for close to thirty years. They are there and we are more than welcome to come up and look at them. It's a funny journey when you're looking for something or someone for a long time. It seems impossible until you find them. Now the easy part . . . hop in the car and go up to see them. So we did, no drama, just a nice long car ride. Pat Curtain, Frank Miklos, and Jim Scott all showed up . . . boat nuts to come to see the barn find of the century. So there we were, right on the edge of summer and fall, looking at the Holy Grail of classic boats. *Thayer IV* . . . in a barn . . . untouched! All of her original parts, the compass, the odd

Diver prepares crash boat for the movie.

Frank Miklos and brother Bob with Mariah.

vent of the front deck, the ladder, books of documents, bills of sale, affidavits—all of it down to the cover pins in the sides. Unbelievable! What also was a jaw-dropper was the US Mail boat used in the movie, a Century Raven, was right there untouched as well. Just sitting there, wondering where I have been.

I fell in love, right there. Like a twelve-ye%ar-old . . . Note here: Chris Smith (of the Chris Craft family), says in his book, and if you ask, that his favorite Chris Craft is a U22 . . . and in my book *Thayer IV* is the best known U22 on the planet earth. And this one, I suppose, is the most iconic classic wood boat in the world. It's the one everyone thinks about when they think of a day out on the water in a Chris-Craft. This boat . . . right here. U22, serial #1460. There is no real way to express one's feelings when in front of the real thing. The truth and the life force that is generated is breath taking. Oh, there are plenty of copies of the *Mona Lisa*, but go stand in front of the real one. That's the magic that happened that day.

Another magic moment was how much we all loved the US Mail boat *Mariah*. And in an odd way, the Mail Boat was there to back up the unknown *Thayer IV*, as if to say, "Hey, we have been here all along . . . Where have you been?"

One thing I learned along the journey here . . . it's the dark side of barn finds. I found out a lot about trust and human nature. I do a website on classic boating. When I broke the story on finding these boats, people cried foul! They did not believe it and started to defend the other boat. Why I'm not sure. They just could not believe there could be another boat.

They attacked me, Pat Curtain, and anyone else that were claiming this boat to be real. As I sat back, I realized that in a sense, we had just corrected history that folks had grown to be lieve. That 1802 was the only boat . . . the crash boat was gone to the dumps and termite poop . . . and now this . . . Who is this guy to claim this . . . Why is he doing it, like I had manufactured the boats. I am not sure I'll do a barn find like that again in my lifetime. The emotional extremes are too much. The highs are great, but the attacks are too low. As things have calmed down, it's fun to know that in a small way, this barn find was one of the moments in my life I'll treasure. The boats are still safely tucked away in a barn. In original condition, now enjoying their life in retirement.

From the Editor: Matt Smith is president of Smith Gifford Advertising. But he is also captain of the ship at Woodyboater.com, America's leading #1 journal for antique and classic boat lovers. My thanks goes out to Matt, not only for his contribution, but for helping design my cover.

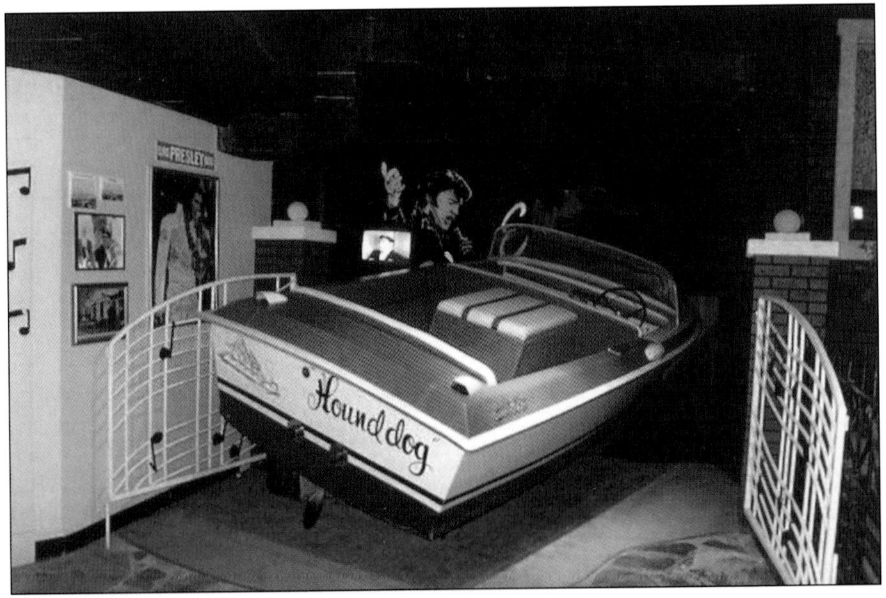
PRESLEY
"Hound dog"

Elvis Lives! In Woodyboaterland

By Tony Begley

ELVIS PRESLEY'S LOVE OF MOTORIZED VEHICLES has been well publicized over time. He obviously coveted almost anything with an engine—cars, motorcycles, airplanes, golf carts. Less known in Elvis lore is his affection for boats. He played a charter captain in the 1962 movie *Girls, Girls, Girls.* However, he also was a boat enthusiast in his personal life. His favorites, of course, were speed boats, and he liked to drive. Decades ago, *Boating Magazine* sent a research team to Memphis to assemble an in-depth history of Elvis and his boats.

They spent months investigating, calling sources, offering rewards for information, interviewing hundreds of people. It was an arduous, time-consuming task. Even today, with the computer and Internet, there's basically no information on Elvis and his boats. This is due to the fact that boating was one type of recreation Elvis and his friends could experience more privately, without fan interference, and he strictly guarded this privacy.

By all accounts, Elvis's first watercraft was *Karate*, a seventeen-foot Glaspar fiberglass ski boat. He and his friends water skied on nearby McKellar Lake. However, Elvis didn't like this boat, and sold it to three members of his inner circle, Memphis disc jockey George Klein, long time pal Joe Esposito, and Alan Fortas. Fiberglass construction of boats was in infancy stages at this time, and there were numerous problems with hull delamination. Frustrated, the trio traded the Glaspar in on a 1963 Chris-Craft Cavalier eighteen-foot speed boat. The *Karate* changed hands several times. Its current location is unknown. The new Chris-Craft was christened *Hound Dog*, after Elvis's wildly popular song. Elvis and friends would get together on Lake McKellar, cruising in *Hound Dog*. Part owner Klein lamented that Elvis liked to drive, but he enjoyed the days of relaxation and sun. Many a shocked boater observed Elvis and friends speeding by them in *Hound Dog*. This was not officially Presley's boat. His name was never on a document of ownership. However, of all the watercraft Elvis was involved with, *Hound Dog* has been identified with him more than any other.

Just a quick digression to the additional boating history of Elvis. He bought two boats from the Memphis Century dealer, one for his father, and one for himself. The whereabouts of his father's boat is unknown. Presley donated his Coronado to the YMCA camp in Arkansas. This boat changed hands several times and was scrapped sometime in the seventies. He also

bought Franklin Roosevelt's former presidential yacht, but soon donated that to St. Jude's Children's Hospital. The research team indicated that, from the mid-sixties until his death, Elvis did not own another boat.

Eventually, Klein bought out Esposito and Fortas to obtain sole ownership. The boat rode the waves on McKellar Lake, sometimes being stored under a carport at Graceland. Klein owned the boat until the late seventies. By then the boat had been neglected and fallen into disrepair. It was sold twice, secondly to a promoter who intended to create an Elvis tourist attraction, but the plan never materialized. Finally, singing star and good friend of Elvis, Jimmy Velvet purchased the boat. Jimmy was not only a friend of Elvis, but one of the world's leading Elvis memorabilia collectors. He operated three Elvis museums in Nashville, Orlando, and Honolulu. The boat was stored in his backyard until he moved it to country singer George Jones's place. Due to lack of space in his museums and the condition of the craft, Velvet put it completely on the back burner.

In the mid-nineties, the owners of the Guinness Museum in Gatlinburg purchased the Chris-Craft from Jimmy. A restoration was performed on the boat, and it's been on display at the museum since. During the restoration, every attempt was made to save original items instead of replacing them, so it did not look like a brand new boat when it was completed. So this is the actual ownership history of the watercraft. Hundreds of people saw Elvis on Lake McKellar in this boat. Thousands have seen it in the museum, and surely some people observed it at Jimmy Velvet's house. Today, the boat is up for sale again on ebay. But if anyone thinks the boat can be dropped it in the water and sail away on it, this is the wrong boat. It hasn't been on the water for years. The engine is with the boat, but it's disassembled and missing components. Still, the boat has great value in that it is a vintage Chris-Craft Cavalier. However, the greater value of this boat lies in the historic significance.

The Legend of Pokey

1954 Chris-Craft - Twenty-Eight-Foot Sportman

By Jeff and Nancy Stebbins

IN THE FALL OF 1954, LUCIAN STRONG, a wealthy man from Wayzata and his wife, Virginia, the daughter of the founder of Honeywell, decided it was time they had a boat to enjoy on Lake Minnetonka. In reviewing the Chris-Craft line, they realized the boat they desired was not available. What they wanted was a large open boat for entertaining, where many people could sit comfortably and socialize. Where Mrs. Strong could arrange the food and beverages to serve their guests. There was also a need for a toilet, and the boat needed to be fast enough to pull their children and grandchildren water skiing.

The twenty-eight-foot Super Semi Enclosed cruiser was the starting point. She was given hull number SE-28-155. Ordered without the hard top, and fitted with a new wood windshield, they had the beginnings of a large open boat for entertaining. On the port side, in the area between the front seats and the engine boxes, they installed an icebox, an ice chest, and a counter top. On the starboard side, they had installed a liquor cabinet countertop and three drawers for miscellaneous items. There was no design for a sink for clean up and to tidy the boat, as there was no need. When the Strongs were going to use the boat, they told the help to make sure there was plenty of gas, food and beverages on board. Everything was taken care of for them. When they were finished, someone else did the cleanup. Up front, the original design remained unchanged with a "V" berth and toilet. The motor boxes were cushioned, and a bulkhead was installed between the galley and engines, allowing for a backrest for lounging on the motor boxes.

What about the water skiing? In 1954, the stock engine for this hull was the Chris-Craft model K, a ninety-five-horsepower motor, clearly not enough horsepower to get the boat on plane and pull a skier. The solution was a pair of model M's 130-horsepower motors. The designers at Chris-Craft said this would give her plenty of speed. And it did. Since my ownership, I have yet to be beaten by a conventionally powered classic. Top speed is in excess of forty miles per hour. This is very impressive for a boat this size and weight. Other options include: speedometer, gas gauge, hour meter, sixty-gallon gas tank, and automatic fire extinguisher. For 1954, this boat was the only one made.

One of the Strong's sons had an endearing name that he labeled most possessions while he was growing up, so why not the new boat. Christened *El Stinko*, the fun was about to begin. The slogan used then was, "Come to *El Stinko* for a drink-O."

The party room on their estate also carried this enduring name.

One might think this boat was the perfect creation for the Strongs. Not to be. The motor boxes were in the way for Mr. Strong, and the walkway between the motors was far to narrow for him. They used the boat for one season. Once again, it was time to visit the folks at the Chris-Craft. This time, the rear deck had to be flush. The only way to accomplish this was to start with a different hull. *El Stinko II* was created from a thirty-foot Chris-Craft Constellation cabin cruiser. They cut the cabin off and made her into a utility. This boat served them for many years.

We have owned *Pokey* for over twenty years now. There have been three owners since the Strongs, and three different names, *Grande Rojo*, *Wood Duck*, and now *Pokey*. *Pokey* is an endearing name I've used in the past, and it somehow fits this boat. You know, as in Gumby's pal.

Nancy & Jeff.

This old Chris has seen continual use on Lake Minnetonka since 1954 until our recent move to Lake Vermilion three years ago. Now totally restored, almost every piece of wood has been replaced. *Pokey* serves us well and gives all who ride on her immeasurable pleasure. She will remain in our fleet forever, as nothing can come close to replacing her.

Editor's Note: Jeff served as president of The Antique and Classic Boat Society of America.

Three Tacos and Hold the Tomatoes

By Rob Schantz
Grand Rapids, Michigan

DREAMS REALLY DO COME TRUE. You just have to believe. I'm an average guy who loves mahogany boats and can never quite seem to get enough of them. Living in Western Michigan gives me the opportunity to visit several people who restore and maintain these classics. When they had the auction at the Chris-Craft plant in Holland, Michigan, several years ago, I went wild and bought as much (stuff) as I could.

Many years ago my father found a 1948 seventeen-foot Chris-Craft Deluxe in a cherry farmer's barn off Torch Lake. The boat had been abused and the barn roof leaked right overhead, but I didn't care . . . I bought it for $500.00. The hardware had to be worth that much. What a learning experience. Everything was toast, but it was a pattern. I replaced the stem, keel, both chines, ribs, transom, bottom, topsides, and shear shelf. It was a process and took eight years. I tried to do as much work on these boats as I could, in order to afford this obsession.

Ten years ago I purchased a 1941 eighteen-foot, six-inch Gar Wood utility in need of a home and a considerable amount of TLC. I couldn't sleep at night until it found our home. I've since sold it to a local club member.

Then in late summer I was finishing off a three-stall garage at our lake cottage, insulating it, dry walling it. On my way out to our cottage, I stopped by this Mexican Restaurant, almost every night. As I was picking up my order at the drive-up window, when the owner said, "Aren't you into old boats?" I said, "Yes!" The owner said "My father-in-law has two old boats. One's seventeen feet long and the other is twenty-eight or thirty feet."

I immediately pulled my car over to the side and went in to interrogate this nice person. My heart was pounding, and I could hardly contain myself. (It also pays to have an A.C.B.S. sticker on your rear window). He said the seventeen-footer was rounded in the bow and in the stern, and didn't have a windshield, and that it was in poor shape. The larger boat was an old "Rum Runner." I would love a dollar every time that term's been used.

I thought I died and went to heaven. The seventeen-footer sounded like my current project, which didn't interest me as much, but the larger "Rum Runner" did spark my attention. After several weeks, this nice person took me way out in the country, down several gravel roads, to an old Christmas tree farm. Of course, the power had been shut off in the barn years ago, but I was prepared with tape measure and flashlight in hand. As he opened the door, I saw over in the corner not a seventeen-foot Deluxe, but rather a 1941, Custom nineteen-foot barrel back. I tried and keep a straight face. This boat just happened to be one of my favorites. The other boat was a thirty-foot Hacker. Gotta love these long "Lincoln Logs." I took another look. The other boat wasn't a Hacker, nor was it twenty-eight or thirty feet long. Although it would have been a great story . . .

Tucked in back of this barn was a 1929 twenty-six-foot Chris-Craft up-swept triple converted into a utility boat when they took out the original power and put a Hemi in it. The doghouse was gone, but most of the "jewelry" was still in tact. The hull was somewhat straight, but it was in need of a total bottom up restoration. The dash in the twenty-six-footer was complete except for the wheel and the shifter. The boat came from an old estate from Spring Lake, Michigan.

The nineteen-foot barrel back was in tough shape, virtually toast. It had been stored inside but was neglected for many years. The boat had absolutely no varnish on it at all. It had most of the hardware, but was missing the windshield, along with the interior, seats, and rub rail. Why was it all old boats needed windshields? "Several" planks had been replaced, and it was virtually a gray ghost, but not a "corn crib." The original power was in it, a model M, and it did turn over. My heart was pounding . . . no . . . they weren't for sale. The owner of the restaurant was considering restoring one of the two and needed to think this through.

I had to put my selling shoes on for Mr. Leonard, the father-in-law, along with very delicate maneuvers at home with my dearest wife. Of course, buying both was out of the question, but I had to have that barrel back. This was the time when I was

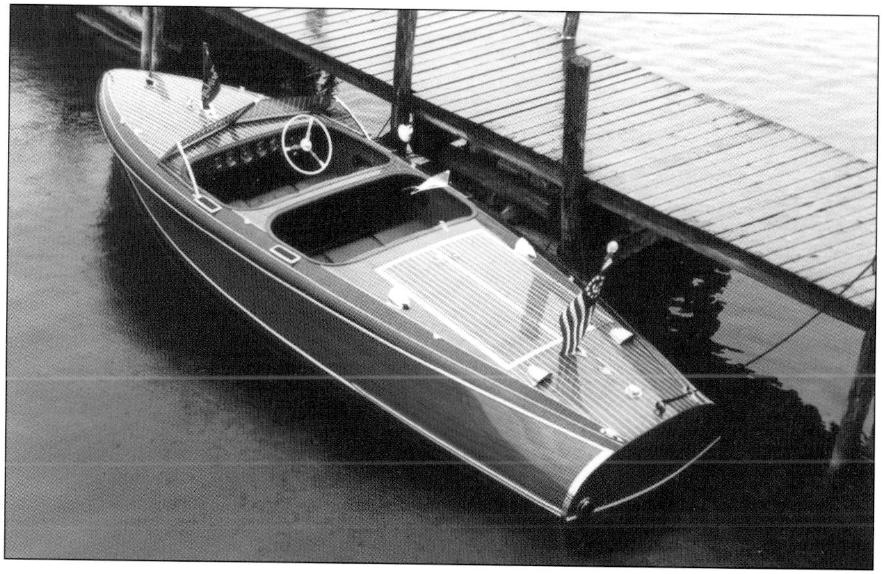

thankful my wife, Barbie, went to boat shows and symposiums. She knew the value of the boat, and how rare it was. I was also thankful for the quality people we'd met throughout our boating experiences, as they were what made this hobby so enjoyable.

Have you ever awakened at night in a cold sweat, and not been physically ill, but maybe a little mentally ill? Try that for several weeks once. With as much patience as I could endure, waiting several weeks, I went back to the restaurant. Without a word spoken, the son-in law, said "Why don't you talk to my father in law. He decided to sell the smaller boat."

Prayers do come true. You just have to believe. After several rounds with "Mr. Leonard," we came to a good agreement.

I finished the 1948 seventeen-foot Deluxe, after eight years, and the boat won best amateur restoration at Traverse City and Hessel. Later that year, we sold the boat to focus on the 1941 nineteen-foot Chris-Craft.

Don Dannenberg featured the 1941 nineteen-footer several times in *Classic Boating* as he did all the planking, topsides, decks and also featured it in his first book. It was one of his first projects after leaving Macatawa Bay Boat Works. The entire boat

was planked using Philippine mahogany. Don planked the boat from one tree, and he took the time to match up the end grain and put the log back together, very impressive. I put fourteen coats of varnish on it and turned it over to Macatawa Bay Boat Work's for the interior, wiring, seats, final coats, and leather. Cadillac Boat Shop helped with some parts and repairs. It's great to live in an area with such quality restorers, I feel truly lucky!

End of the story . . . not quite. My restaurant friend's father-in-law passed away several years back and the 1929, twenty-six-foot Chris Triple became available. I purchased it too. It came with 150 gallons of porcupine droppings, along with a live porcupine. Have you ever tried to get a live porcupine out of a boat, short of getting the twelve guage out? Just remember . . . mothballs. I grabbed its tail with gloves . . . but that's another story.

You always hear the stories that today there aren't the boats in barns or boathouses like there use to be, but I can attest they are still out there.

Remember one thing . . . the next time you order a meal. That waitress, waiter, or restaurateur may be the ticket to a great dessert!

Wood Is Good, But Glass Is Class

By Del VanEmmerik

FIRST, SOME HISTORY ABOUT FRP—Fiberglass Reinforced Plastic. Fiberglass was around long before the boat-building boom of the 1950s. Owen Corning was making fiberglass airplane parts for the war effort in 1942. Possibly the first fiberglass boat, a sailboat, was built in 1942.

By the 1950s fiberglass was on its way! The boating industry took to FRP like a duck to water.

Glass boats helped open the market to millions of boaters who did not have time, money, or patience to maintain a wood boat. Glass was the beginning of the end for the wood boat industry. Glass boats could be made cheaper and faster, and with little structure maintenance for the owner.

Fiberglass boat building was fairly easy to accomplish. Thus, the reason literally hundreds of new boat builders sprung into being. Many of these builders had a very short life span. Some as little as a year or two. With some companies producing a dozen or even fewer salable boats. The exciting part of all this is that many of the boats constructed of fiberglass have survived. No matter how badly they were neglected.

This brings us to the story of the carAqua boats and Marine Plastics, Inc., 825 Northwest Eight Avenue, Fort Lauderdale, Florida.

Marine Plastics applied for its carAqua patent in 1957. The company had a production run of only two years, 1958 and 1959. Little is known concerning the actual number of boats built. To this day only eleven are known to exist.

Marine Plastics produced three different models, the V.I.P.,the Runabout and the Station Wagon.

The V.I.P. model (Vertical Inboard Power) had a forty-five-horsepower Crosley four-cylinder power plant called a Fageol engine, which stood on end and was placed inside under a trunk-like cover at the rear of the boat. This boat boasted twin automotive style side mirrors and headlights that could "Turn

night-time into day-time" with the flick of a switch. Only one, very rare V.I.P. is known to exist.

The Runabout. Marine Plastics kept to its car theme on all three models. The Runabout model had a split cockpit with a walk-through and featured molded front and rear seats. Other features included headlights (with a dimmer switch for high and low beam), wraparound windshield, tail fins to the back sporting working taillights, ski hooks, and a faux grill decal between the headlights.

The final model was the Station Wagon. The Station Wagon still had the outside options of fins, lights, windshields, and grill, but was toned down some on inside, with only one bench seat in the front, leaving the rest of the boat open back to the transom. This boat was more a Marine Plastics utility style boat. It seems that this model may have sold the most as there are seven of these boats out there.

Having ridden in and driven all three models of the carAqua, I can tell you tht they handle rough water and waves

very well and are fun to go boating in. And, further, the carAquas are one of the most popular '50s fiberglass boats for the collectors.

The Runabout model carAqua is outfitted with a pair of 1963 forty-five-horsepower McCulloch Scott outboards similar to the boats of the fifties and sixties. These outboards have a long and interesting history.

In 1932, Cliff Scott and H. Bruce Atwater had a successful punch-press operation going. They were approached by a gentleman to build him a small outboard motor. This motor was a real success story and, thus, the Champion outboard was born. Scott and Atwater built these motors and kept their punch-press operation going until 1939, when they switched to building outboards only. With the outbreak of World War II, production of these outboards ceased, and their expertise turned to helping the war effort.

After World War II, in 1946, Firestone continued its association with Scott and Atwater and was back in the outboard market.

Scott (Scott-Atwater) is noted for many engineering breakthroughs. They were the first to produce a line of "full shift" motors. (Forward-neutral-reverse). No more turning the motor 180 degrees to get reverse.

Scott is revered for the invention of its Bail-A-Matic in 1954. This was a small metal foot placed inside the boat and connected to the motor via a rubber hose. When the engine was running, it produced suction and any water that had leaked into the boat was sucked up and removed.

One more innovation by Scott was its Shallow Water Drive. By moving a lever in the cockpit, one could trip a pin on the motor and allow the lower unit to tip up six inches, making it easy to motor through shallow water or to pull into shore. When finished with the shallow water drive, one simply moved the lever shift into reverse and the lower unit would settle down into the original position.

By 1958 Scott-Atwater motors were called Scotts or Scott McCulloch, but in 1964 all motors became McCullochs. Sometime in 1969, McCulloch stopped all production of outboards.

Over the years Scott-Atwater built:

Firestone for Firestone (1946-1957)
Hiawatha for Gambles (1956-1959)
Corsair for Phillipp's 66 (1948-1957)
Elgin for Sears

The 1961 75HP motor was the largest motor produced.

The name brand McCulloch is still in business to this day. The McCulloch chain saw is just one of its products.

Mahogany Monogamy

Or, the Man Who Loved One Boat

By David Kanally

"I have been here before!" exclaimed my mother as she and my father approached the waterfall along Six Mile Creek. "I used to bring campers here when I was a counselor at the camp up the road." This unexpected connection to her past brought my mother fully into the excitement of the day. The journey had begun with a very different intent . . . to trace the origins of Cowell Boat Works, the maker of my father's 1957 sixteen-foot outboard runabout.

The waterfall on Six Mile Creek.

Although the Cowell name is still known in Erie, Pennsylvania, Cowell boats are all but forgotten. The family's standard bearer today is Richard Cowell, an attorney practicing in Erie. His late father, Tom, was the founder of Cowell Boat Works. Richard had invited my parents this day, and graciously accompanied them on a probe into his family's history.

Richard Cowell and one-boat-man Dek Kanally.

Cowell Beach, accessible only by the Cowells' private drive, which my parents. Their Erie friends, the Sorces, hesitantly followed them through the vine-laden woods. They reached the two-story frame home where Richard grew up, and proceeded toward the bluff that overlooked the beach.

They passed a cottage and a barn, and then saw Richard gathering and burning driftwood on the beach. He climbed the bluff to greet them and showed them around the property, including its own natural wonder, the waterfall along Six Mile Creek.

They gingerly picked their way down a steep path toward the beach where Richard and his wife, Jane, had been clearing the driftwood. There, massive concrete slabs and reinforcing steel that once were a boat slip and pier lay askew, victims of forty years of Lake Erie freezes and thaws. And a bit farther up the beach were the crumbling remains of the buildings where Cowell boats were made. Doors and windows were long gone. The paint was splotchy. The vines and bushes that dominated the property were well on their way to reclaiming these buildings as well.

Cowell Boat Works in its Heyday

Thomas Cowell had been building wooden boats at his home for about a year, largely for the boat livery trade. He had experienced sufficient demand to expand operations and employ several craftsmen.

One of those young craftsmen was Ron Smith, who honed his woodworking skills on the mahogany gunwales and decks of many boats, including the one that my father would one day own. Ron, who has been building homes in Erie for the past twenty-five years, cited this early work experience on the home page of his construction business website. It was this single Internet reference to Cowell Boat Works that opened the door for our discovery of Cowell's history in the summer of 1999.

From Richard's family archives came brochures that detailed the various models in the Cowell line. "Sea Pups" were the open fishing boats used with small engines, driven from the stern. Our boat was clearly one of the runabouts, a "King."

The old pier and Cowell Boat Works buildings in 1999.

New Boat Industry Sprouts

June 6 · 1954

By LEN KHOLOS

Erie is known throughout the world for the diversified products manufactured in its environs, and now another local son is steadily placing the city on the map for yet another industry.

Thomas Cowell started building boats a year ago at his home at the mouth of Six Mile Creek.

His success promises well for the employment future of the community. Cowell has announced plans for construction of a new plant that will employ from 20 to 25 men next spring.

• • • •

A June 1954 newspaper article proudly announced the expansion of Cowell Boat Works.

Dek at the stern of the Cowell's nineteen-footer, June 1999.

Other materials from Richard included a publicity photo made in the late 1950s with employees, neighbors, and friends aboard, including young Ron Smith at the wheel.

Completing their tour of the Cowell property, my parents saw a late 1950s Cowell nineteen-footer, sheltered in the Cowell's barn since it came from the shop.

But our family's Cowell boat story began over a decade later, in 1969.

The Muskrats and Boat Ownership Peer Pressure

Our first encounter with Cowell boats was unintentional. Sometime early in the summer of 1969 we decided that boat ownership was desirable. Our family, together with three other families known collectively as "The Muskrats," had shared a summer rental cottage on Bemus Bay at Chautauqua Lake, New York.

Throughout these summers, the kids of all four families spent most of their school vacations at the lake. The parents, who had responsibilities to their work, rotated the weekday kid-sitting burden, each couple taking their turn watching all the kids during one week of the summer. On weekends, though, everyone from the first and second generations of Muskrats was at the lake.

In the early years, we had access to one boat, a Penn Yan sixteen-footer with a gutsy Johnson sixty-horse belonging to Phil and Jewell Meacham, the senior Muskrats. Behind this boat, every young Muskrat learned to water ski. Soon thereafter, our bright red, square-stern, fiberglass canoe, the *Muskrat*, joined the flotilla. No perch or bluegill was safe from a junior Muskrat dropping his line over the gunwales of this stealth craft.

Not to be outdone, fellow Muskrat H.S.J.B. (more about him later) added two crafts to our Navy: *The Ramstuk*, (can you find the word Muskrat therein?), a featherweight oak and plywood rowboat, and *Remister II*, a tiny sailing tub named after H.S.J.B.'s horse. (H.S.J.B. was born and raised in Boston, but lived and kept horses in Pennsylvania). No other Muskrat had horses or sailboats, so it was good for us that H.S.J.B. was in our midst.

This floating frenzy culminated in a trip to the Starbrick Marina in Warren, Pennsylvania, by my father, my younger brother, Kevin, and me, in June of 1969. We drooled a bit over the new-looking and new-smelling boats in the showroom, but our budget led us quickly to the back parking lot where, sitting alone and sorely neglected, was a blistered and peeling wooden runabout of noble lineage. A swooping script logo, "Cowell, Erie, Pa." was affixed to the rear hull, on the port side. We immediately saw the potential and overlooked the shortcomings of the slightly shabby craft. A few hundred dollars later, we drove off with the boat, a forty-five-horse Mercury outboard and a Cox trailer built for the millennium. (Thirty-one years later, all three items would prove themselves to be Y2K compliant.)

When we pulled into the driveway, my mother's expression let me know that no parental pillow talk had preceded this

Kevin Kanally effects the first restoration, 1969.

The Muskrat, the olds and young Muskrats David, Kent and Kevin in 1969.

purchase. This "Honey, guess what!" buying technique has served me well over the ensuing years.

We set straight to the work of restoration. A stained blister on the front deck plywood was injected with glue with a veterinarian hypodermic needle, pushed flat with weights, then sanded. All topside surfaces received several coats of spar varnish. The hull was painted with white marine enamel. In short order, the new old boat was ready for launch.

H.S.J.B., denatured alcohol, and the "fish-pound" theory.

"Handsome Smiling Jerry Bozzo" he signed his cards and letters. An engineer by training and a corporate executive, gentleman farmer, building supplies retailer, and horse owner by profession, H.S.J.B. had knowledge of most subjects, especially those involving mechanics, electronics, chemistry, boats, dock building, and horses.

This knowledge impressed us young Muskrats deeply, and came in particularly handy on the day we launched the new old boat.

The Launch and the Sputter

Hesitantly, with multiple re-orientations, we backed the trailer down the public boat ramp at Bemus Point. The fresh varnish reflected the upstate New York partly cloudy skies. The fresh, new American flag fixed to the stern light snapped in the lake breeze. After the ceremonious shove-off, we cranked the Merc, and she turned over just as she had done at the Starbrick Marina. My brother, my buddy Kent (elder son of senior Muskrats Phil and Jewell), and I were to pilot the boat back to the cottage.

But then our hearts sank. The motor would run only at half throttle. We chugged around the bay a bit, pulled the cowling from the motor and pretended to adjust things, to no avail. Dejected, we returned to port and trailered the boat back to the cottage.

The fateful first launch, 1969.

H.S.J.B. to the rescue. His expert diagnosis revealed that the lower carburetor was clogged with "vahnish," the dried residue of the 28:1 gas/oil mixture that the 1960 power plant burned. He also determined that denatured alcohol would make a suitable solvent for said varnish, because it was "sufficiently volatile." We young Muskrats accepted this diagn%osis at face value.

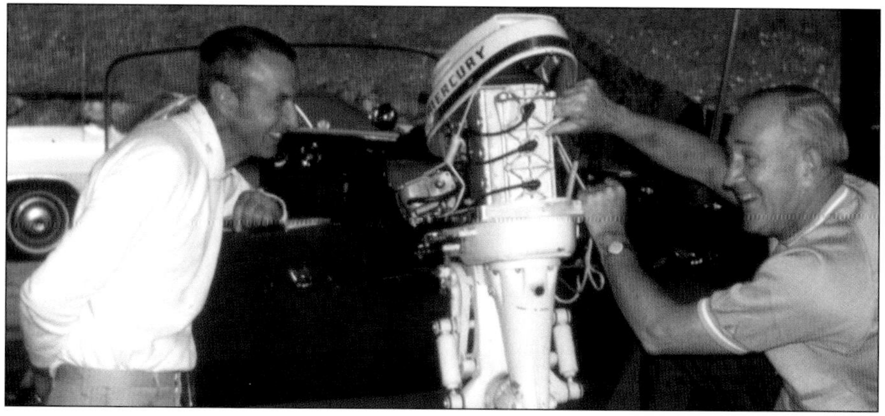

H.S.J.B. and Senior Muskrat George "Casey" Case (who left this life way too soon) on the day of the carburetor miracle.

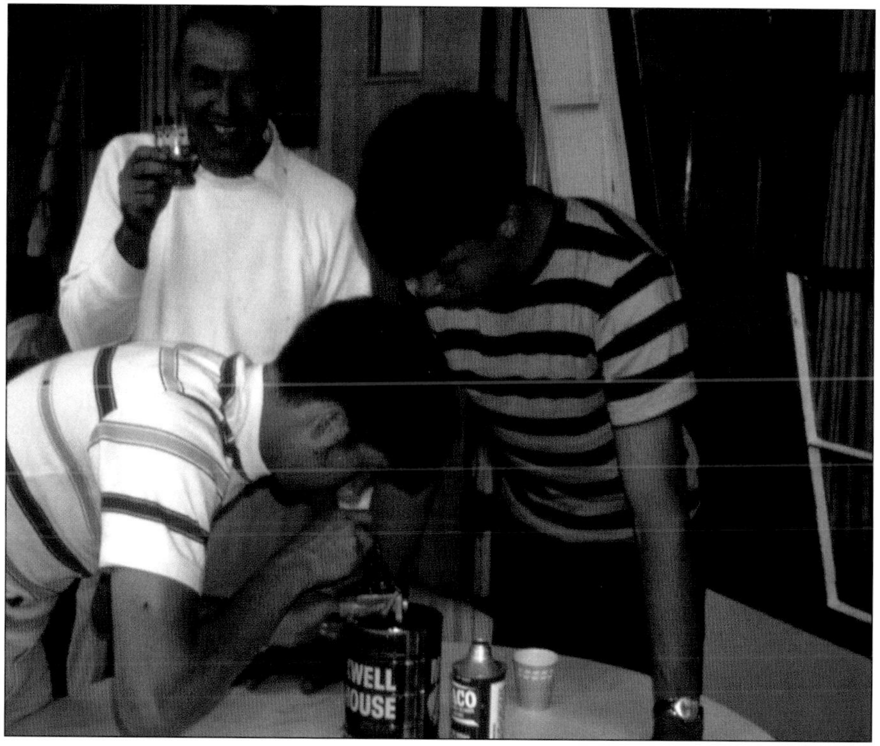

Kent and David ream the carb jet with denatured alcohol while H.S.J.B. conducts a volatility evaluation on a Manhattan, 1969.

With youthful bravado and close coaching by H.S.J.B., we pulled the lower carberator, dismantled it and reamed out the jet with a denatured alcohol-soaked broom straw. Following careful reassembly and remounting of the carburetor, we dragged a fifty-five-gallon drum to the stern of the trailered boat, pulled the drum up and around the lower housing of the motor, and filled the drum with water. This time, the Merc not only turned over, but whined into the highest rpm range, churning and spewing water like a possessed eggbeater. We were mechanics! All thanks to H.S.J.B.

The "Middle Years" and the Mortician

As young Muskrats grew into adulthood, the Chautauqua summers came to an end. The new old boat was due for another restoration. The blister on the front deck had risen again, and the stains just seemed to get worse and worse. We were understandably concerned for the boat's health, but nothing could have prepared us for the day the mortician showed up. What relief we felt when it became clear that Frank Switzer wasn't there to bury the boat, but to improve it. You see, in a town the size of ours, there aren't enough people dying to keep a mortician busy full time. So Frank laid tile and did upholstery on the side. His solution to our blemished front deck was to cover it with a high-quality nut-brown-colored vinyl upholstery material, which he did, quickly and masterfully. Seats, gunwales and other remaining woodwork received numerous new coats of spar varnish, and the new old boat was ready for the middle years.

Empty nesters Kanallys, Delacours, and Paynes cruising Kippawa Lake, Quebec, 1981.

Since we kids were grown and gone, my dad used the boat for two main purposes: to take a couple of other people's young kids fishing at Chautauqua Lake from time to time, and to travel with my mom and several other empty-nest couples to Kippawa, Quebec, for week-long fishing trips.

At some undocumented point during this period, the boat and trailer both received a coat of cream-colored paint to match the new Olds station wagon.

Hagar's Magnificent Obsession

Something came over my father in 1985. He had a vision of a completely restored new old boat. He began a process which would fill our garage, consume his time and challenge my mother's patience for nearly two and a half years.

At some point during this time, my mom began calling my dad "Hagar" after the boat-loving Viking of comic strip fame. She laminated and displayed Hagar comic strips on the wall of the garage as her quiet vigil continued.

A hardy band of guys led by Bob Hartle, our town's second underemployed mortician, came to help Dad flip the boat so he could begin removing the multiple coats of paint. With a heat gun and scraper he spent evening after evening scraping through layers and layers of cream, white, green, yellow, and other colors of enamel until he reached bare wood.

Once the scraping phase was complete, the guys re-righted the boat. Dad removed the troubled front deck entirely, and replaced it with brand new marine mahogany plywood and trim he had to drive nine hours—all the way to White Plains, New York—to get.

For all the Hagar teasing he got, it's important to note that my dad is a skilled and fastidious woodworker. He boiled and bent new oak ribs to replace the rotting members in the stern.

My father-in-law, Ken McLaughlin (who also left this life way too soon) and our sons Eric and Brian atop the partially scraped hull, celebrate Dek's progress in 1985.

Dek plugs screw holes with bungs, 1987.

He designed and built new gas tank holders and created a new seat to cover them. He raised the rear seat to accommodate both cranking and accessory batteries. He plugged screw holes with bungs, trimmed them with a tiny Japanese back saw and sanded everything until it was perfectly smooth.

He acquired all these products by mail order, and painstakingly applied them all to his new old boat.

Troubled Trip to Texas

Hagar (the boat, not the Viking) made a few trips during the years between 1987 and 1999 . . . mostly day trips or weekends to Chautauqua Lake or Kinzua Dam. Lately, though, the new old

Dek and H.S.J.B. inspect the new mahogany front deck, 1987.

The result was a mahogany jewel, glistening with a mirror finish.

boat had been in storage most of the time, and my dad thought it was about time to pass it along. I was thrilled at the prospect of being the new owner of the boat, but one major logistics challenge lay ahead . . . how to get the boat from Pennsylvania to Texas in a time-efficient and economical way.

After considering several options, we decided that it would be best to acquire my brother's 1988 Isuzu Trooper (which he was looking to sell anyway), tow the boat to Dallas, then sell the Trooper. Our elder son, Brian, and I would do the driving.

Good plan, but the Trooper didn't have a rear bumper, and the hitches locally available in Pennsylvania required one.

So we had to add a supporting member to the rear frame of the Trooper to support the hitch. This modification held up for the first 250 miles of the trip, getting us to the west side of Akron, Ohio, Medina to be precise. At that point the rusting rear frame gave way, and we needed the intervention of some professional welders to reinforce the hitch to make sure we could finish the remaining 1,200 miles of the journey.

We found a welding shop that would do the work, which caused a half-day delay in the journey, but only a minor blip in

Mom and Dad launched the boat at Kinzua Dam near Warren, Pennsylvania, where Mom officially christened the boat Hagar.

Brian and David: Texas or Bust, June 1999.

Hitch solution #1.

Hitch solution #2.

the project budget. We finished the trip without further incident and found a new home for the new old boat in North Texas.

Finding the Good Life in Texas

Since coming to Texas, the Kanally Cowell has become affiliated with the Antique and Classic Boat Society (ACBS) and the Wooden Boat Association of North Texas. The Cowell has been in several shows, including the Texas State Fair, the Annual WBA Show & Ride at Lake Lewisville, and the Annual Keels and Wheels show at Clear Lake.

The boat that one man loved is now safely in the loving care of another. The new old boat is plying the new millennium in ship shape. The new owners are thankful that Dek's craftsmanship and care have made this all possible.

New coat of Epifanes spar varnish, November 2000.

A Spectacle of Spray and a Touch of the Daring!

The Story of the Flying Boatmen

By Steve Early. Photos courtesy of the Jim Early Collection

The decade of the 1950s produced a character in boating not seen before or since. The charm of those unique hull designs with eye-catching curves and sleek spray rails revealed an age of expression, right down the mahogany flag posts. In those days, simplicity reigned supreme and nowhere was this more apparent than in this unforgettable era on the water.

Boating in the 1950s began to take on the appearance of imagination and color. Vessels were pure vintage complete with a "tail fin" look that conveyed an innocence now seemingly lost forever. This decade of boating offered "the look" of personality with a hint of performance. These were the good ol' days many of us dream of getting back to. Imagine multiple, yet identical, classic crafts amplified across the water some twenty times! That is exactly what the Flying Boatmen of Knoxville, Tennessee, brought to audiences for over two decades.

Conceived in 1953 by an Air Force colonel, the Flying Boatmen Club was the nautical answer to the aeronautic shows still performed today by the 'Thunder Birds" and "Blue Angels."

Colonel Scott Fellows, stationed at Knoxville's McGhee–Tyson Air Base, imagined the possibility of performing maneuvers such as echelons and diamonds, but executing these formations on water instead of in the air. He had quite an original idea, so in 1953 he took his vision from paper to pond. Fellows knew a concept of this caliber needed help plus a little luck along the way, and sure enough, his first big break came in the form of an introduction to a fellow named Dixie Loy. A marine store sales executive, Loy knew all different types of boats, numerous potential drivers, and the many east Tennessee lakes. Fellows had the concept, but Loy had the commitment over the long haul to make the Flying Boatmen a household name in east Tennessee. Fellows would move on in due time, and over the years, it would be Loy's unwavering dedication and matchless connections that would propel the Flying Boatmen to national prominence.

With Fellows concept, and Loy's contacts, the search was on for the right hull capable of handling rough water punishment without sacrificing maneuverability. The answer: The Feather Craft Vagabond . . . a lightweight V-hull aluminum boat featuring a rudder from bow to stern complete with the "tumble home" curved sides. It was this distinctive design which provided an unmistakable look from the grandstands and an unbeatable performance from the driver's seat. Feather Craft had the product and the Flying Boatmen never strayed away. In over twenty years of active performance, the club never found another hull that offered all of the intangibles of the Vagabond. The Feather Craft made the Flying Boatmen . . . and sadly, it brought on their demise. When the Vagabond model was discontinued in 1959, the Boatmen were on borrowed time.

But in 1953, it was all systems go as Loy assembled a number of enthusiastic boatmen from Knoxville. The original Flying Boatmen drivers came from all walks of life: a police chief, a home builder, a TV news man, auto mechanic, factory foreman, tour bus driver, and upholstery manufacturer give an idea of the career diversity represented in the club.

But the author of this story can tell you first hand of one trait these great men all shared: They were SUPERIOR drivers, and even better people. All of them. History tells us the original Mercury astronauts represented "the best of the best" and the original Flying Boatmen drivers took on a similar quality. No weak links in the bunch! While many of these unique and colorful individuals have since passed on, yours truly has had the pleasure of being on the water with a number of these gentlemen and has witnessed the split second timing and their matchless high-eye coordination with the throttle. These men could put a Feather Craft into a space others wouldn't dare. They could span the river lined up only inches apart running full speed . . . and never flinch. These guys were good. And their shows were even better.

If you ever saw the Flying Boatmen perform, you would remember the spine-tingling image on the horizon of multiple Feather Crafts emerging like an army, show flags proudly waving in the breeze, an impressive "Big V" of Vagabonds growing larger and larger as the formation approached the show area. "A spectacle of spray and a touch of the daring!" the show's emcee would exclaim. And on any given day, fans would be

treated to a fleet of Feather Crafts ranging from nine up to seventeen boats depending upon driver availability. (Club rules maximized the membership at twenty-five). Following the introductory Big V formation, the Boatmen would blend a majestic, soothing formation with the excitement of split-second timing by means of the "Vagabond Parade." This popular maneuver featured the boats in two columns approaching the shore at full speed, only to peel back and criss-cross at the rear of the twin column. It is difficult to describe with the word. You simply had to see it. Through decades and literally hundreds of shows, the author is only aware of two collisions of any significance. Both occurred during the Vagabond Parade.

Again, this incredible safety record is a tribute to the quality of the drivers and the hours they committed to practice, year after year after year. After the Vagabond parade, the Flying Boatmen would break into multiple groups and showcase many of the traditional diamond, echelon, and small "V" formations their Air Force ancestors made famous. Then it would be time to show off the incomparable turning radius of the Feather Craft

by creating an "Old Western Wagon Wheel" and even a classic full speed Figure 8! (And it was no maneuver for the faint of heart).

The Flying Boatmen would then build the moment for the climactic close by pushing the Feather Craft to its performance limit. One unique quality Fellows and Loy may or may not have bargained for in the Vagabond was its ability to literally "spin-out" at full throttle and change direction with a massive show of spray and thunderous roar of the outboard motor. In this instance, the steering wheel is rapidly turned hard all the way in one direction while the bow of the boat digs in causing the stern and prop to come completely out of the water. The bow and stern swap ends, then the entire hull rocks back down in the water as if dropped from a two story building. (The author strongly discourages any attempts of this particular maneuver, and if you're thinking of attempting such a stunt in a Feather Craft Rocket, be prepared to go swimming). The spin-out provided an exciting close to the show that literally brought spectators to their feet time and time again. "Split the Hair" always quickened the pulse of the audience as two boats would proceed downstream, a single boat upstream with just enough room to pass between the other two. Once through, all three would perform a wide open "spin-out." It was quite a crowd pleaser.

The end of the show featured each boat performing a single spin-out close in to the audience on the shore line, followed by "double spin-outs" with two boats spinning simultaneously, and finally, the hair-raising triple spin-outs executed with amazingly few feet separating each boat. Total run time of a performance averaged forty five minutes to an hour.

Down through the years, only one thing has ever been known to top the grace, precision, and excitement of seeing these Flying Boatmen shows—and that's seeing the Flying Boatmen at night! That's correct. The Flying Boatmen rigged their Feather Crafts with special frames of multi-colored lights and performed these identical stunts after dark. "Spectacle" does not do it justice. Imagine the difficulty of running such close maneuvers in broad daylight, only to turn around and demand the same precise patterns, and at times when the only ray of navigation light is coming from the moon. Somehow, someway, the Flying Boatmen always pulled it off.

With the club being based in Knoxville, local crowds were treated to regular performances, particularly downtown between the bridges, exactly where the popular Vol Navy gathers today for University of Tennessee football games. But the club loved to take their act on the road, and it was never for money. The Flying Boatmen toured with their families and their boats, all for the love of boating, nothing more. In their hey day, the club was nationally recognized and sought after by a number of communities and boating clubs. The Flying Boatmen resume included such stops as Lake Michigan in Chicago, Fontana, North Carolina, the Potomac in Washington, D.C., Poplar Bluff, Mis-

souri, Atlanta, Georgia, Silver Springs, Florida and other aquatic destinations. Even their caravans on interstates and highways were show-stoppers. This parade of colorful blue, gold, and silver Vagabonds stopped traffic everywhere they went. Entire families were outfitted in special white Flying Boatmen oxford button downs with embroidered red canvas jackets (and in the early days the drivers sported the classic black captains hats). If you were a child and your parents were in the club, as was yours %truly, you enjoyed a fun and memorable childhood.

Many assume the club got its name from its close kinship with the Air Force "Thunderbirds," but that is not the case. In the early days of the club, the Boatmen were performing on Lake Allatoona near Atlanta. During a planned spin-out, an excited reporter from the *Atlanta Journal Constitution* exclaimed, "My gosh man—look at those Flying Boatmen!" and the name stuck.

If you were fortunate enough to be voted into the club, you then had to pass weeks and months of driver training before any consideration was ever given to performing in a live show. And if you did not own the complete package of Feather Craft boat, Johnson outboard, and Gator trailer, you were automatically disqualified. These were the brands associated the Flying Boatmen. Another key element Loy brought to the club was the staunch support of these three companies. From its inception to its last performance, Feather Craft, Johnson, and Gator were exclusively used and endorsed by the Flying Boatmen.

Another name synonymous with the Flying Boatmen was "charity." The big-time drivers were also known to have big hearts. Fund raisers for organizations too numerous to mention were a consistent deed performed by the club. Many a special needs child experienced the ride of their life in the incomparable Feather Craft Vagabond. Their ear-to-ear grin was all the satisfaction the drivers and their families ever needed.

Many of those special rides took place in Knoxville on the fair grounds known as Chilhowee Park. A very modest man-made "lake" provided barely enough depth for the Vagabond hull to make dreams come true for many kids, big and small, young and old alike. It is amazing that one of the most enduring memories the people of east Tennessee have of the Flying Boatmen are their boat rides in Chilhowee Park. Given its tight quarters and shallow draft, it's possible those rides may be the only ones ever experienced on that body of water . . . and only in a Feather Craft.

Another body of water navigated expertly by the Flying Boatmen was the wild and winding Ocklawaha River near Ocala, Florida. This was boating at its finest featuring all the thrills and tight turns of a roller coaster.

Given the narrowness of the channel and the unpredictable S turns in the river, most vessels could take this stretch at no better than half-throttle. The Feather Craft was the proven exception. Some incredible color motion-picture film from the

late 1950s captures the Flying Boatmen "skating" the Ocklawaha at full throttle speeds. (Skippers beware: For this river, you never want to get caught on the outside of another boat's rooster tail (wake) when taking a tight turn. In the blink of an eye you could go from "Flying Boatman" to "Flying Bankman"). The Ocklawaha became a favored destination of the club throughout its life span. Not surprisingly, it was the discovery of Loy.

In 1981, some five years after the final show, the Flying Boatmen held a reunion at their familiar club house location lake side in the Louisville community of east Tennessee. (The club house remained and was maintained by a couple of the surviving original members until sometime in the early 1990s when it was donated to charity). On this day in 1981, the author remembers seeing all of his childhood Flying Boatmen heroes through the eyes of an eager teen-ager, having just arrived at the realization of being born too late. It's true, I missed the hey day of the Flying Boatmen but came along just in time to see a number of shows and experience the "Spectacle." I was eleven years old the last time they performed an official show. Now I was sitting at the reunion with my parents listening to my Dad (former driver and always the emcee) introduce a lot of the famous names and faces associated with the club.

As he approached the end of his speech, Dad predictably saved his best line for last . . . "And ladies and gentlemen it gives me great pleasure to recognize MR. FLYING BOATMAN . . . Dixie Loy!"

With that, I witnessed Mr. Loy, once a proud, stocky, powerful man now weakened by old age and a stroke, become emotional over his introduction. At that very moment, I remember thinking there would come a day when I would regret not being able to hear his amazing story of the Flying Boatmen recalled in his own words.

Let me assure you. That day has arrived.

ABOUT THIS AUTHOR: Steve Early is the son of former Flying Boatman, Jim Early (driver and show emcee from 1955 to 1972). He lives in Knoxville, Tennessee, and is the owner of four (4) Feather Craft Vagabonds, including his father's original show boat. Two of Early's Feather Crafts, both 1959 models, are in prime showroom condition with minimal hours of original use. Early fulfilled many of his childhood dreams throughout the late 1980s and 1990s by cruising with several of the original Flying Boatmen drivers in a number of their famous formations.

Evinrude Outboards, 100 and Still Going Strong

By Dennis Evinrude

THE YEAR 2009 MARKED the 100th anniversary of the outboard known as Evinrude. The humble beginning of this business is also a love story. After spending a number of years working throughout the Midwest, Ole Evinrude came to Milwaukee in 1900. The twenty-three-year-old had gained valuable knowledge in various foundries and machine shops and was ready to create on his own. Ole's first endeavor was to build engines that allowed people to convert their carriages to self-propelled units. Ole had just been kicked out of a boarding house run by a Mrs. Doyle who had a sixteen-year-old friend by the name of Bess Cary. Adjacent to the Cary property was a shed for rent, which Ole did. Ole took on a partner and formed a company to custom build engines for whatever people desired. At the same time a curious Bess volunteered to type correspondence needed to start the business. Her reward was an occasional horseless carriage ride and Sunday picnics. The firm of Clemick and Evinrude lasted only six months, but the relationship of Ole and Bess would endure through thick and thin. After enjoying many picnics together, Ole and Bess were engaged in the summer of 1906. Near the end of that summer, they and a few friends journeyed to Lacys Resort (now the Golden Mast) on Okauchee Lake and rented a boat for

Ole Evinrude

Bess Evinrude

the trip to Party Island. During the course of the day Ole returned to Lacys to fetch some ice cream for the group. On the return trip, Ole rowed into a stiff wind and the delay caused the ice cream to melt. The frustration of the melted treat set into motion events that would change outboard history in a big way. Bess encouraged Ole to develop an affordable engine that the common man could clamp onto any rowboat he wished.

On November 21st, 1906, Ole and Bess were married. On September 27th, 1907, their son, Ralph S. Evinrude was born. After Ralph was born, economic times were tough and Bess's health suffered. They persevered and by the summer of 1909 Ole had an engine ready to test. Ole and Bess's brothers took the engine to the Kinnicinnic River, clamped it to a boat, and off they noisily went. Many people rushed to the riverbank to see that historic event. At this point Bess's influence on the company also made history. She had the foresight to see the market possibilities and the business acumen to make it happen. Many years later Ole and Bess would both remark how they were the perfect business partners as well as perfect partners in matrimony. Bess ran the office and created all the advertising while Ole ran the shop and saw to it that reliable outboards were produced. The engines developed 1½ horsepower, weighed sixty-two pounds, and initially sold for $62.00.

After five very successful years, Bess's health suffered again. Ole did what some men might regard as radical today. He sold the company and concentrated on restoring Bess to good health. They traveled the country and among other places visited my Dad's (Ole's brother) family home in Glendive, Montana. My father is ninety-five now and still remembers their visit. By

1920, they settled in New Orleans where Ole and young Ralph worked on a new engine design together and Bess grew stronger.

In 1921 their new engine took the New York Boat Show by storm and entered full production in 1922. Due to the sale of their original company, they did not have the right to use the Evinrude name, so Bess coined the acronym ELTO (Evinrude Light Twin Outboard). Once again the advertising and business genius of this lady propelled the company forward. One must realize that for much of her career women in the United States did not even have the right to vote. All of her correspondence was signed "B. Evinrude." Only those who met her in person ever knew they were dealing with a women. Bess was a trail-blazer in the truest sense. The Elto Company was very successful while the original Evinrude firm was slowly failing. In 1929 Stephen Briggs of the small engine maker, Briggs & Stratton, approached Ole, and together they formed a new concern which consisted primarily of the original Evinrude and the new Elto companies. Thus, OMC was born.

Four years later Bess's health deteriorated again, and she passed away on May 13th, 1933, at the age of forty-seven. The love that had made the perfect partnership was now a dark void. Those who knew Ole well say he was never the same and a scant fourteen months later Ole passed away on July 12th, 1934. He literally died of a broken heart. From the time they started the most successful outboard company ever to the time of their deaths was a mere twenty-five years.

Their son Ralph took over OMC and, under his direction, survived the Depression, supplied the military with outboards during World War II and guided it to worldwide success well into the 1980s.

Today, the Evinrude E-Tec is produced by Bombardier and is the only outboard to date to win the EPA's "Clean Air Award." Things have come a long way since the love of two talented people brought forth a brand of outboard engine that celebrates its 100th birthday.

1958 Crestliner Voyager "Adelaide."

A Family Classic

Often Passed Down through Generations, the Crestliner Voyager Has Staying Power

By Lee Wangstad

TUCKED AWAY IN A CRESTLINER dealership in Little Falls, Minnesota, sits an almost perfect example of a boat that came to exemplify family boats of the 1950s. *Adelaide*, a 1958 Crestliner Voyager, was returned to Monahan's Larson Motor Service by a relative of the original owner in 1988. Never launched, it still showed signs of being brand new. "The bottom of her hull has redwood sawdust (shavings from the seats) and aluminum grindings along with the nails from pop rivets from the day she left the assembly line," said John Monahan, one of the owners of Monahan's Larson Motor Service.

The boat still sits on its original Tee-Nee trailer, its bright yellow paint contrasting sharply with the red bottom of the flawless boat. If you look at the transom closely you can detect marks where a motor was once attached, but the motor had been given to a neighbor of the owner long ago.

Adelaide was most likely purchased in anticipation of hot summers spent relaxing on the water, a dream that would never materialize. For one reason or another, the boat would never leave the garage, the engine would never run, lazy days on the lake would wait for another day that wouldn't come. While to some it may seem a waste, a dream that could never come alive, it has instead left us with an artifact that is still intact, original in its entirety.

At a time when boating was just entering the mainstream of American life, the Voyager, at its 1954 debut, pulled Crestliner into competition with larger manufacturers with a full model

1955 Crestliner Voyager.

lineup. It gave Crestliner a true family type runabout with a windshield, deluxe seating, deck hardware, all the features necessary for fun on the water. Originally introduced as a fifteen-foot convertible, it was also later available as an eighteen-foot model in either a convertible or hardtop.

All three models provided extraordinary room with a full-width bench seat at the front cockpit, twin opposing seats running the length behind the cockpit, and another full-width bench seat at the stern. While these redwood seats looked nice, passengers were encouraged to bring along seat cushions to help smooth out the ride. The 1954 and 1955 models are easily identified by their tall split-V windscreens, and the 1956 and later models by their wraparound windshields. These windshields were of the no-nonsense, keep-the-spray-out-of-your-face variety, not just a styling gimmick or glitzy ornamentation.

With the exception of the 1957 Voyager hardtop, the color scheme matched the rest of the Crestliner line: red decks and red bottom, with the hull sides left in their natural aluminum finish or, as in the case of *Adelaide*, painted silver. The aluminum available after the Korean conflict had a yellowish stain to it, and it was more affordable to paint it than to purchase a higher grade of aluminum. The 1957 hardtop was painted white with green accents, an indication of styling changes taking place at Crestliner.

As Crestliner changed its lineup in 1958, it produced more fully painted boats, new models that were larger and more comfortable. The eighteen-foot Voyager convertible and hardtop models were dropped, replaced by the roomier Flying Crest model. Still available was the fifteen-foot Voyager runabout, now joined by a fourteen-foot model formerly called the Viking, upgraded to Voyager status.

The year 1959 would prove to be pivotal at Crestliner with the introduction of a line of fiberglass boats. In 1960, with this fiberglass line expanding, the Voyager faded away, replaced by the

1957 Crestliner Voyager Hardtop.

1958 Crstliner Voyager-like Adelaide.

From the 1958 Crestliner Catalog.

fancier fiberglass rigs with more options, accessories, and comforts.

Testimony to the Voyager comes with the fact that so many of these boats are still are still on the water today, giving their owners (either old or new) the same recreational value that they were meant to when new over fifty years ago. They have been either lovingly maintained by original family members or painstakingly restored by a new class of owners that still enjoy the rugged durability and classic good looks that are what these boats are all about.

About This Author:

Lee Wangstad was born in Minneapolis, Minnesota, but spent his summers at his parent's summer cabin on Waverly Lake, forty-five miles west of Minneapolis. Lee is probably best known for his Classic Boat column that appeared in *Boating World* magazine for over fourteen years. His writing has also appeared in *Classic Boating* magazine, *The ACBS Rudder*, *Lake Country Journal*, *The Boathouse*, and the *Antique Boat Museum Gazette*. He has spoken at numerous symposia, including the 1997 ACBS Antique Motorboating Symposium in Newport News, Virginia;

Lee and his all-original 1959 Larson Thunderbird.

the 2001 and 2005 National Boating History Sympoia in Cincinnati, Ohio; and the 2008 Wet Edge ACBS International Boating Symposium in Seattle, Washington. He has been a featured speaker at numerous ACBS chapters, including the Bluegrass Chapter, Bob Speltz Land-O-Lakes Chapter, the Buckeye Chapter, Chesapeake Bay Chapter, Greater Cincinnati Chapter, Indiana Chapter, Pacific Northwest Chapter, as well as participating in the 2005 Seattle Garage Tour.

The "B" Words

By Brian Fanchini

WE ALL TALK ABOUT HOW the restorable number of wooden boats is starting to dwindle. The barn-find legends and abandoned boathouse myths are fun to dream about, but are they really just that, myths and legends? While it is true there were a finite number of wooden boats produced, and a large majority have been found and restored, there are still enough left in hiding to make every enthusiast's heart jump when they hear the words "boat" and "barn" uttered in the same sentence.

Such was the case on a warm summer evening in 2007 when my son, Cole, and I were launching my Tollycraft for a lap or two around Lake Tapps. I live across the street from the lake and use a good friend's private launch just a few houses down from ours. Greg is a bachelor living the lakefront dream and regularly has a deck full of guests during the summer. As I backed my boat into the water, one of his guests leaned on the deck rail watching us intently. I just assumed he was marveling at my flawless launching skills (on the third attempt) or the fact that my eight-year-old son can handle dock lines like a pro. Instead he yelled down to me, "I've got an old wood boat in my barn you might be interested in." Might be interested?! He must not have realized he used both of the B words in the same sentence. With me trying not to seem too eager, we spoke for a few minutes and exchanged phone numbers for the following day. He did know that it was a Correct Craft and it was a plywood boat, but other than that, it was just an old wood boat in his barn.

I spent most of that evening and early hours of the next day on the computer trying to make myself knowledgeable about Correct Crafts. The company was founded in 1925 by Walt C. Meloon and originally called the Florida Variety Boat Company. In 1936 the name was officially changed to Correct Craft. They built boats that ranged from fourteen-foot runabouts to fifty-five-foot cruisers. Great! That really narrowed down my focus. Needless to say, there was not much sleep that night and

I fought off the urge to call the owner at 6:30 a.m. "Might be just a little too early. I'll let him sleep until at least 6:45."

I made arrangements to be at his house around 10:00 that morning. Cole and I arrived at his farm, armed with a camera and all my newfound Correct Craft knowledge. From the driveway, we could not even see the barn, which just made the anticipation even more unbearable. It really is difficult to carry on a casual conversation with someone when you really just want to push them out of the way and run for the barn! He had warned me that it was a project boat so I wasn't expecting too much when we finally walked around the house and into the field. What stopped me in my tracks though were the lines on this little chunk of wood. I got started in this hobby by rebuilding a vintage fiberglass finned boat and have a special place in my heart for the rocket-inspired fin designs of the late 1950s. So to see this tiny wooden boat complete with wooden fins was more than I could take. Running up and hugging a boat was not the preferred bargaining method, so in my best John Wayne type slow drawl, I asked, "What do you think you want for it?" I almost peed when he replied that the barn space was more valuable to him than the boat, and I could have it if I'd try and rebuild it someday.

An hour and a half later I was back with a flat-bed trailer and loaded up the boat and all the miscellaneous parts. I marveled at the boxes of parts as I loaded them. Each part was tagged with a small note as to where it had been on the boat. At the bottom of one of the boxes was a file folder stuffed full of original Correct Craft factory photos and manuals. As we were freeing up his barn space, he told me that his dad had bought the boat from the original owner in the early 1970s. On his first trip with the new boat, he had hit a submerged log in the Columbia River and tore off the raw water intake. The boat sank at the shore before they could get the trailer back under it. He brought the whole boat, complete with the raw water intake that was still hanging on the bottom back and put it in the barn for the next thirty years. A rebuild was started in about 1995, but only made it to the hardware removal stage. With a little research, I found that the boat was a 1959 Correct Craft Atom Skier Deluxe. The Deluxe had fins; the standard had none. The boat was complete, including a seventy-horsepower Universal Unlimited four-cylinder flathead and all of the hardware. I was currently working on the research to ensure the finished boat represents the original as closely as possible.

Factory Photos

As most boat stories go, this one does not stop here. While searching the dreaded ebay one night, another Atom Skier popped up. At only $1,000 with ten minutes left, what could be

the harm in bidding? The next weekend, my dad and I made a whirlwind trip from Seattle to Los Angeles and back to retrieve a second little Atom. This one, a 1960 version with a Graymarine V8-188, had a story all its own, but suffice it to say a 327-horsepower engine stuffed into a fourteen-foot boat was just too much to pass up! As soon as the funds make themselves available, this one is going to Rob Dapron's shop so he can work his magic.

My imagination still gets the better of me when I pass a barn leaning to the side from years of resisting gravity. The old boathouse that season after season is never open still raises my curiosity. I even find myself getting excited about cyber hunting boats on the computer into the late hours of the night. But none of these seem to compare to just two simple words, boat and barn, spoken together to really get our attention.

The Return of the Rusticator

By John Allen

After calling this Maine Island boathouse home for eighty-three years, it's time for the Fay & Bowen to move.

TIME WAS LESS COMPLICATED IN 1923. Cars were black, shirts were white, and ice cream was vanilla or chocolate. Flappers danced to the Charleston, and Americans listened to "Yes We Have No Bananas." The nation was also discovering boating, and manufacturers like Chris-Craft, Hacker, Garwood, and Belle Isle were gaining national prominence, producing affordable mahogany speed boats, whose popularity and desirability were driven by exploits and racing records of dynamic personalities like Gar Wood, Horace Dodge, and Caleb Bragg.

The city of Geneva lies at the northern end of Seneca Lake in the fabled Finger Lakes Region of New York State. There the Fay and Bowen Engine Company, manufacturers of marine engines and pricey "gentlemen" powerboats of considerable reputation and distinction since 1900, accepted a signed order from internationally known archeologist and collector Dr. J. Howard Wilson of Binghamton, New York, and Castine, Maine. The preserved original order and specification contract, dated March 28, 1923, documents the purchase of a thirty-foot runabout launch, design E-36, with a fifty-horsepower LNS-43 Fay and Bowen engine.

This distinctive launch, commonly called a Golden Arrow, (the twenty-six-foot versions were Black Arrows) was designed by Navel Architect Morris M. Whitaker of Nyack New York and was introduced by Fay and Bowen in 1920. The Golden Arrow commanded a purchase price of $3,800.00 plus tax. Fay and Bowen marketed the Golden Arrow as a family runabout that was modeled along cruiser lines with a high free-

board providing adaptability for heavy weather without looking "tubby." Company advertisements claim the Golden Arrow was one of their "smartest" boats. Its name derived from the gold leaf arrow that ran from the stern to the bow. The gold leafing of the arrow was a $200 option.

Other specifications included a five-foot-six beam, a twenty-three-inch draft, a cruising range of 150 miles and a promised top speed of twenty-one miles per hour. White oak was used in the keel, ribs, stem, and engine bed stringers with copper and brass fastenings. Mahogany comprised the coaming, plank sheer, interior finish, decks, and hatches. All deck hardware was polished bronze, and the seats and laybacks were upholstered in high-grade leather. Two coats of antifouling green copper paint were applied to the underbody and the freeboard was a smart, white gloss finish.

Fay and Bowen was required by contract to deliver the boat in the compressed time frame of seventy-five days. The rapidly approaching summer of 1923 was likely on Mr. Wilson's mind, and it seemed he was quite intent on joining the other wealthy, vacationing Eastern seaboard families of Castine for stylishly dressed afternoons of rest and relaxation on Penobscot Bay and other waterways of the resort area.

J. Howard Wilson, and other wealthy summer vacationers to northeastern Maine, were mockingly called by the locals and press "Rusticators," because they came to Maine from urban areas to enjoy the "rustic life." However, their summers were not without the trappings of comfort and convenience such as cooks, butlers, maids, nannies, big cars, and, of course, expensive boats.

In compliance with the contract, Fay and Bowen stamped the bill of sale paid on June 16, 1923, and shipped the runabout launch named *Najoqui* from its Geneva factory to Rockland, Maine, for a "wharf delivery" aboard the Maine Central railroads grand trunk car #32347. *Najoqui* then traveled by water to its waiting boathouse in Castine, immediately across from the owners' Nautilus Island estate. *Najoqui*, last licensed in 1984, resided safely inside this coastal Maine boathouse for over eighty-three years.

Boat collectors recognize Fay and Bowen Golden Arrows as extremely rare. At eighty-seven and cruising toward its 100th birthday, *Rusticator* enjoys unusual stature even within this exclusive class for a number of reasons. One, it's still powered by its original factory LNS-43 Fay and Bowen Engine. Two, the hardware, gauges, underbody, freeboard, and steering are preserved or restored originals. Three, the boat's providence is enhanced with the original contract, marketing specifications, packing list, wiring diagram, engine manual, bill of sale, and bill of landing. Lastly, Wooden Boat Specialist of Clayton, New

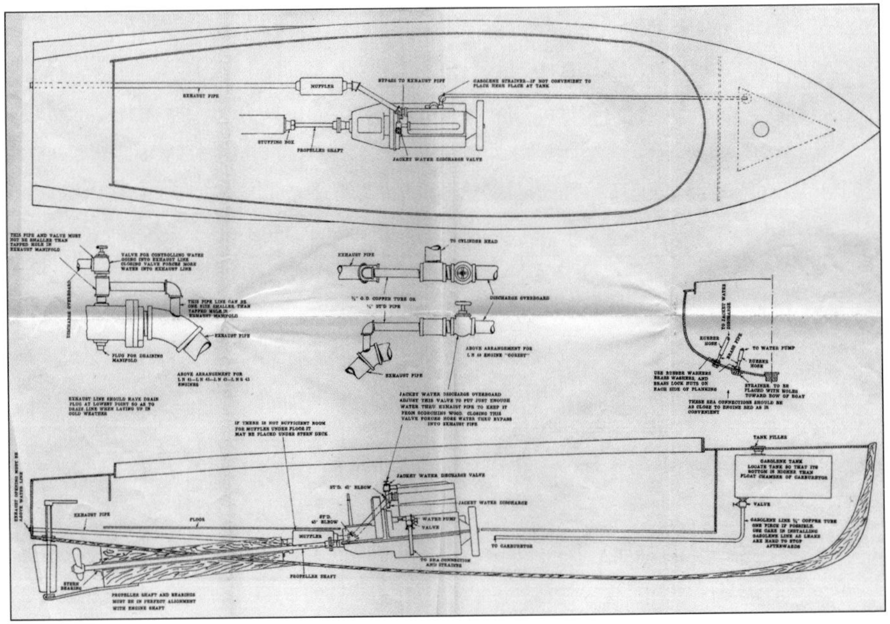

DANGER

Rusticator
1923

York, has done a historically faithful restoration of the interior, deck and upholstery to Fay and Bowen factory specifications and standards. Likewise, Bill Drake and his team of engine doctors in Rochester, New York have beautifully reconditioned the Fay and Bowen LNS-43 engine.

In a fitting acknowledgement of the boat's historical Finger Lakes connection, *Rusticator* debuted at the Finger Lakes, Skaneateles Boat Show in July 2009, proving that, despite the old adage, you can come home again. After Best of Show wins in Skaneateles, New York, Clayton, New York, and Hessel, Michigan, *Rusticator* was selected as 2009 International Antique Boat of the Year Restored at the ACBS International Show in Gravenhurst Canada.

The sleek and graceful cooper and brass laden lady *Rusticator*, a true survivor from the Golden Age of Boating, now slides gracefully through the waters of Gull Lake, Minnesota, with the family and friends of collectors John and Becky Allen, enhancing the summers of its second family while historically connecting them to a dramatically different time, in a dramatically different country.

Outboard Addiction

By Jim Seufert

I GUESS THE AFFLICTION REALLY STARTED in about 1965. I wasn't old enough to drive, but my best buddy died and his dad let us borrow the car. Grandpa let me borrow his 1955 Wizard Super 10, so we went up the creek (literally) to an old marina that was willing to rent an old fourteen-foot tinny to a couple of kids. Five bucks for the whole day! It was usually half sunk, so the first hour was spent bailing her out. By the end of the summer, Grandpa saw how good I was taking care of the old girl, so he gave me the Wizard. he had sold the boat a few years earlier, so he waas happy to see her back in service again.

A few years later, Grandpa moved to a different house and for the first time in his life he had a garage—a big ol' double. That fall, Grandma died and Grandpa was a little lost. By then, I was in college and had a few extra bucks from a part-time job, so I suggested we use the garage to build a boad. A carpenter by trade, Grandpa was onboard without hesitation.

The sixteen-foot Luger plywood kit cost $165 delivered. The first step was assembling the keel, stem, and transom. That was the first problem! Do we cut the transom outto fifteen feet to fit the short shaft Wizard? We thought it wasn't a good idea, so we decided to set the transom at twenty inches till the finances would allow a long shaft motor (and a bigger one, too!) Now that I look back, I had the kicker before I had the main!

The ol' Wizard did indeed become the kicker. Right next to the brand spanking new 1968 Evinrude Lark. That took a little help from Dad to make the payments!

Fast forward through graduation, marriage, and a family.

Now we needed a bigger boat. The upgrade was an I/O and Grandpa's old Wizard went with the trade. Looking back, selling the Super 10 was the worst mistake I ever made.

Fast forward again—now the kids are out of the house and have boats of their own. Retirement is still "out there," but now it's at least in sight. The extra three-car garage was built in the backyard with the intention of either building another boat or finding a nice restorable classic.

Then, there she was . . . one just like Grandpa had. We got the 1952 Lyman home and started the restoration process right away. She came with a 1953 Evinrude Big Twin that needed not much more than cosmetics.

That fall, my father-in-law passed away, and I inherited his Martin, along with Great-grandpa's matching model. They were bought together in 1948 and were only a few serial numbers apart.

A chance stop at a garage sale a few months later netted a 1955 ten-horsepower Johnson, complete with two suitcase tanks for the massive sum of twenty dollars. It even ran!

Now the obsession started. Estate and garage sales, eBay, etc., etc. Joined the AOMCI. My prize motor is a 1920 Model A Evinrude Rowboat motor, bought from the original owner, who hung it on his garage wall after he used it last in 1951.

The affliction continues, and I haven't even retired yet. The count is now up to sixty-one. My wife calls my garage the "museum." I simply call it the "boathouse."

When Grandpa was alive, he was my inspiration. Anytime there was a new motor, a new boat, or simply a new piece of hardware added, he got the first ride. Now I blame it on all you guys in the AOMCI. It *is* an addiction. But I wouldn't have it any other way.

The Cobra on the Farm

By Bob Matson

With permission of *The Fargo Forum* newspaper.

ONCE AGAIN, I REMIND YOU that the inspiration for this book came from a book about cars. Tom Cotter's *The Cobra in the Barn*. I talked to Tom after reading his book and I told him I had an idea for a book about finding old boats in barns. He jokingly said to me, "Wouldn't it be amazing if you got a story about finding a Chris-Craft Cobra in a barn?" Well, that's just about what happened!

In searching for great stories for this book, I knew I would have to talk with major boat restorers. One day, on a whim, I called Tom Juul, a well-respected boat restorer in Minnesota. After hearing what I was looking for, he said, "You have to call a guy in Fargo . . . he's got a great story to tell. He found a Cobra on a farm!" I almost passed out.

I immediately asked where and he says, "Near Oakes, North Dakota."

I screamed, "I used to live in Oakes while managing a radio station there in the '70s! I might have walked right past it while pheasant hunting!

I thanked Tom and, with shaking hands, called one Dave Selvig of Fargo, North Dakota. After hearing his story, I knew I had a great chapter for the book. I'll try to do justice to what information was sent me, most from articles by Erin Hemme of the *Fargo Forum* newspaper. The odyssey started long ago . . .

When Dave Selvig was a lot younger, he spent summers at his grandmother's cottage on Lake Sallie near Detroit Lakes, Minnesota. There he puttered around with an Ole Lind wood boat with a five-horsepower Mercury motor. Many summers were spent around old wood boats, even a Falls Flyer. These memories lay dormant for many years, though, and it was much later that Dave got the bug. They say a boat finds you, not the other way around. The first restoration project came in the late seventies when he rescued the family's Ole Lind boat. It was basically a scrape-and-paint job. Nothing too impressive there. But it was many years later when he was driving down a new street in Fargo that took him past a construction yard of an acquaintance. Something caught his eye. It turned out to be a 1948 Century Deluxe Utility. That's when the bug really hit him. He made the deal and completed the project with much help from the likes of Bob Speltz and Tom Juul. Over time, Dave and his helpers completed more project boats. (Why is one never enough?) He restored a 1959 sixteen-foot Cruiser, Inc., and a 1960 Seaskiff with a 283 that he found in a shelterbelt by East Grand Forks, Minnesota. Then came the Cobra.

Chris-Craft
'93 4 2

One day in 1992, a local marine dealership in Fargo got a call from a family wondering if they would want to buy the family's old wood boat. The owner said no, but to send him pictures and he would show them to a friend of his to see if he would be interested. That person would be Dave Selvig. When Dave finally saw the Polaroids, his heart skipped a beat. "I looked at the photos and nearly fell out of my chair", says Selvig. To an untrained eye, it looked like a pile of rejected firewood. To Selvig, it was a collector's dream, the kind that makes collectors drool. He instantly recognized it as a 1955 Chris-Craft Cobra, one of only 108 made. The Cobra had been sitting in a field near Oakes, North Dakota, for seventeen years. Now the family wanted to sell it, but they had no idea what it was. They thought they had an old worthless Chris-Craft ocean racing boat. But Dave knew there was no such thing. The owner, who lived in Texas, was happy to sell the dilapidated boat for $1,000 because he thought he had a pile of junk. "I'm glad I didn't have to negotiate face to face with the guy," said Selvig. He could hardly keep from jumping up and down! The deal made, and Dave made plans for him and his wife, Bonnie, to travel to Oakes to pick up the boat.

When they arrived with much anticipation, the farmer led them to a feedlot, and there, resting in the weeds, snuggled in tall grass, was the unmistakable signature of a grand lady begging to be discovered. The fin, standing at attention, minus the Chris-Craft insignia, seemed to be waving at anybody who would catch a glimpse and rescue her from the waving weeds.

What is known about the boat is that it was originally delivered to Kampeska Marine in Watertown, South Dakota, in 1955 with hull number 41. No record as to the original owner or subsequent owners. This is the original, signed equipment record sent to the Marine dealership.

Original Polaroids sent to Selvig.

History of the Cobra

Why all the hoopla over this boat? It wouldn't hurt to give a brief history of the Cobra and why it is so rare.

After World War II, and with the resurgence of the economy and changing attitudes, cars were taking on a fresher look.

This picture had writing on it that said—
1954 Cris-Craft ocean racing boat!

To keep up, the boating manufacturers looked to the colorful and stylish cars, some now made of fiberglass, like the Corvette. For companies like Chris-Chraft, now located in Cadillac, Michigan, this meant experimenting with this new material too. So in 1954, the company designed a boat with it's first fiberglass section: a sculpted, golden dorsal fin on the Cobra. It was a classy marriage of mahogany and plastic, but the public shunned the boat. With only a single seat and a hefty price tag of $4,000 to $6,000, it was clear that this was not a family boat. It gained a reputation as only a boat for "the snobbish rich person."

Because of its negative reputation, Chris-Craft cancelled production after only one year. According to Chris Smith, grandson of Chris-Craft founder, Chris Smith, the Cobra did attract attention and brought buyers into the showroom where they bought more practical models. Only four of the 108 Cobras made ended up in the upper Midwest. Hull #41 was delivered to Watertown, South Dakota, and later wound up in that field near Oakes.

Restoration Process

Acccording to Selvig, he found the restoration process to be a real challenge. Because it was abandoned for so long, he was

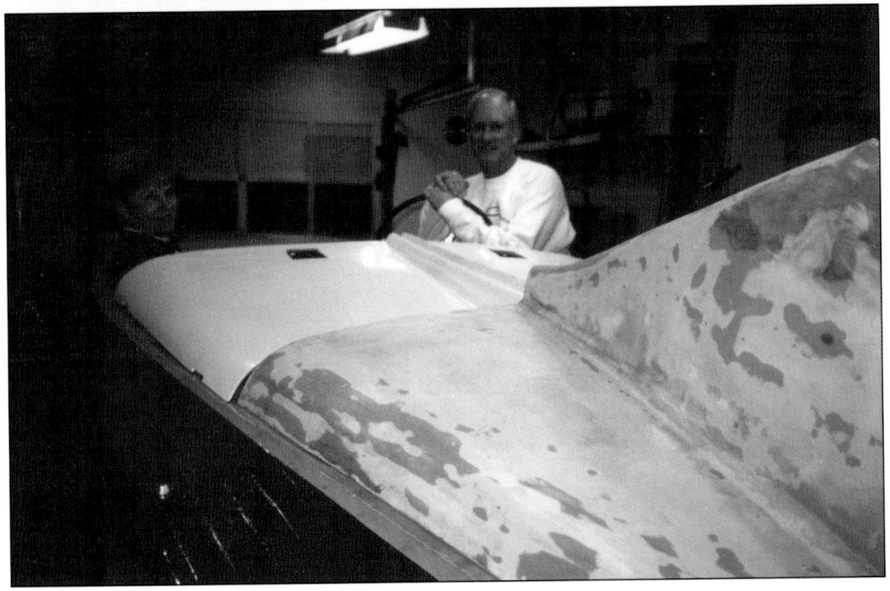

The restoration begins.

Beautifully restored Cobra Hull #41.

only able to salvage two major wooden pieces from the original boat—the engine stringers, which run from the bow to the stern. Every other piece was carefully removed, copied and recut from mahogany or white oak. "There's no way I could do this by myself, and it would not have happened if it weren't for Tom Juul," said Selvig.

Even though the boat was not fully restored, the Juuls and Selvigs took a memorable trip to the fortieth reunion of the Cobra in Cadillac, Michigan, in the summer of 1995. Though there were forty Cobras at the event, none drew more attention than hull #41. It was an archeological find for the Chris-Craft aficionados. "People were climbing all over it, taking pictures and measurements," said Selvig. The boat received the distinction of "most in need of restoration."

Terry Fiest, of Orlando, Florida, and president of the national Cobra Club, said "His boat is a phenomenal story . . . left there to decay and he just stumbled on it. That doesn't happen much any more."

Can't Beat the Sound

Like other boat collectors, it's the sound of the inboard motor that he liked best. "There's nothing like it in the world!" said Dave. That's because the motors don't have mufflers and a tail pipe directs the exhaust into the water. It generates a deep gurgling sound similar to the sound of a Harley-Davidson motorcycle.

The boat has been fully restored, and in fact, has been sold to a new owner and now plies the waters of Lake Placid, New York. "It's taken awhile to restore, but for me it's a hobby" said Selvig. "When I took it out on the lake, it turned heads. People see this torpedo-shaped boat that looks as though it originated from a science-fiction movie . . . ninety-five percent say they have never seen anything like it, and they wonder if it's new."

Back in 1955, only 108 Cobras were made and today eighty of the boats have been found. For collectors who still want to find one, the Cobra remains elusive. You could win the lottery much more easily. "It's one of the more collectible post World War II boats," said Jim Wangard, editor of *Classic Boating Magazine*. "If I found one, I'd sure hope the seller doesn't know what it is."

With new owners on Lake Placid, New York.

The Boat House

By Eric Matson

With a twist of a key and the click of a lock, I open memories of this old shed by the dock.
Though planks are split and weathered, the floor soaked with oil, year after year it waits undaunted, steadfast and loyal.
The paint is dry and peeled, the windows cracked; propped up by logs, it leans slightly to the back.
The morning sunlight streams in through the door, illuminating the memories a lifetime spent in store.
The warm smell of gasoline aged in the wood, brings to mind thoughts that no other place could.
Fishing poles hung together, the new and the broken, are a testament to time, powerful yet unspoken.
Some trips were better and others worse than the last, and the boat house stands witness to the season of our past.
In time honored tradition it holds guard in this way, always gazing quietly over our corner of the bay.

To Grandpa and Grandma with love.

Mystique and Memory

What Is It about Wooden Boats That Enchants Us?

By Bob Matson

I'M OFTEN ASKED, "WHAT IS the mystique of old wooden boats?" Dennis Evinrude said, "If I have to explain it, you probably wouldn't understand. For some of us, it's in our DNA. For others, it's the appreciation of a fine work of art, the engineering, design style, and craftsmanship. These floating sculptures all have a story to tell." Back in the early days, when someone would buy an original watercraft, its builder would also build an elaborate custom boathouse to shelter the treasure, because the value of the boat was generally five and sometimes twenty times the price of a new automobile. Only the very wealthy could afford them. That exclusivity, of course, now translates into rarity.

In October 2010, F. Todd Warner set the bar for bringing this "mystique" back to life by auctioning off over 125 wooden boats, bringing in almost four million dollars. The event was billed as the "awakening of an American treasure." Todd's passion was to keep these boats in as original a condition as possible. "If you were to replace the legs on a Chippendale table or a Sheraton sideboard, you would destroy the value," he explained.

Back in the 1960s, wood boats were considered just about valueless. Some resorts would stack them up and burn them just to get rid of them. Warner refers to this period as "the first harvest of classic boats." Today, when seeing and hearing a wooden boat on the water, we can feel transported back in time and marvel at the workmanship its owner preserved. Especially prized are boats crafted by Minnesota builders like Dingle Boat Works, Moore Boat Works, Wise & Sons, Garwood, or Larson Boat Works.

There is a special place where boats like these can be viewed up close. It's the Minnesota Lakes Maritime Museum in Alexandria, Minnesota. If you have a boat show in your area, it would be worth your time to take the kids and show them how majestic boats were made before their time. It might spark their passion for wooden boats, and if all goes as planned, their lifelong love of classic boats will keep the wooden boat community strong for generations to come.

Boat Class Definitions

- **Historic** – built prior to 1915
- **Antique** – built between 1916 and 1942
- **Classic** – built between 1943 and 1975
- **Early Contemporary** – built between 1976 and 25 years from present
- **Late Contemporary** – built between 25 years from present to present
- **Runabout** – engine under deck and does not have a passage between seats
- **Utility** – engine enclosed in a box (dog house) and has a passage to walk around engine
- **Lapstrake** – planks overlap each other as opposed to smooth side
- **Cruiser** – primarily designed to sleep aboard
- **Outboard** – engine mounted on the transom, outside the boat
- **Row Boat** – no power other than oars
- **Original** – still has all it's original equipment as shipped from the factory

WILDERNESS ADVENTURES
ELY, MN
WILDERNESS OUTFITTERS
CAMEL
LAND ROVER
UPG
9 F

About the Author

"I was born on a dock and wrapped in swaddling camouflage."

Bob Matson is a veteran radio and television broadcast executive with many diverse talents and experiences. He served as an on-air personality as well as manager and sales manager of several radio and television stations in the Midwest. Bob later served as executive director of the North American Bear Center and host of *The Bear Facts* radio show. Today, he owns Matson Motors Marine & Small Engine Repair, specializing in vintage boat and outboard restorations. He is a columnist for *The Timberjay Newspapers* and *Minnesota Moments Magazine*, featuring vintage boats of the north.

When not feeding wild bears out of his hand, he carves wood fish and bears with his chain saw.

He is a member of the Antique Outboard Motor Club, Inc. and the Bob Speltz Land O' Lakes Chapter of The Antique and Classic Boat Society, Inc.

Bob and his black Labrador, Walleye, live on a remote lake near Ely.

I'll go anywhere to get a good story

Every boat has a story. Your boat could be in my next book! If you think you have a great story, like the ones you've just read, I'd love to hear from you. I'm particularly looking for those "rare" stories that are supported by before and after pictures.

If you or someone you know has a story to tell, I can be reached at rcmely@frontiernet.net or by writing me at 203 Cedar Lane, Ely, Minnesota, 55731.

My Favorite Links

To find out more about classic boating, visit some of my favorite sites.

www.whatsinyourboathouse.com

www.woodyboater.com

www.retrocrestliner.com

www.bslol-acbs.com

www.aomci-com

www.acbs.com

www.thetimberjay.com

www.minnesotamoments.com

www.snapper.com

www.jonsered.com

www.Hondalawn&garden.com

www.wolfland.net

www.nelsonboatworks.com

www.sunriseriverboatworks.com

www.rivaforum.org

www.sierraboat.com

www.antiqueboatsales.com

www.elyecho.com

Acknowledgments

I have so many people to thank for this book, I don't know where to start. Of course, I want to thank those contributors and their wonderful stories without which this book wouldn't be possible. But there have also been people for which I give special thanks. They would be Jim Brandenburg, for providing the cover photo of the Stuntz Bay boathouses on Lake Vermilion; Matt Smith of Woodyboater.com, for not only designing the cover, but also for promoting this book on the website, and for sleuthing out the second story of the *On Golden Pond* boat; Tom Kotter and his great book tht gave me the idea in the first place; Ann Stewert for cleaning up my manuscript before submitting to the publisher; Tony Mollica, Jr., and Lee Wangstad for mentoring me andoffering up much support; Dave Schmidt, who put together my website; and, of course, North Star Press and the entire crew there, who had such faith in me.There are many others, and if I have omitted your name, please know I am grateful.